HAUNTED EXPEDITIONS
IN THE MIDWEST

MELISSA CLEVENGER AND CRAIG NEHRING

CONTENTS

About the Authors

Melissa Clevenger joined Fox Valley Ghost Hunters in March of 2018, and she is the lead investigator for the team. She is the coauthor along with Craig Nehring of *Archives of a Ghost Hunter II.* Melissa has been on numerous podcasts throughout the United States and UK, such as *The Midnight Society, The Ghost Host,* and *Hillbilly Horror Stories,* just to name a few. In June of 2020, she was featured on Destination Fear on the Travel Channel featuring the Sheboygan Insane Asylum. Melissa has devoted much of her time to investigating the unknown. The paranormal is a part of her life and a part of who she is.

Melissa was born in 1979, growing up in Marquette, a small farming community in central Kansas. Her experiences with the paranormal started at an incredibly young age. She would always see ghosts and they would communicate with her.

Melissa now lives in Sheboygan, Wisconsin, with her husband, Travis, and their three kids (Taylor 19, Kaleb 7, and Colton 6). She has traveled to countless notorious haunted locations checking off her bucket list. Delving into the history of the locations that she investigates intrigues her. Through the years her ability to see ghosts has faded, but her passion to communicate continues.

Craig Nehring grew up in the Minocqua area where he graduated from Lakeland High in 1988. He was an avid water skier for local ski clubs in the area. He lived only an hour away from one of the most haunted mansions called Summerwind, which he would visit during his high school days. This led to his interest for the paranormal. Craig is the founder of Fox Valley Ghost Hunters, a team that covers all of Wisconsin and the Upper Peninsula of Michigan. He is coauthor of *Wisconsin's Most Haunted Vol 1 and 2* and author of *Archives of a Ghost Hunter,* Volume 1. He is coauthor with Melissa Clevenger on *Archives of a Ghost Hunter,* Volume 2, which was released in 2020. Craig has been heard on radio shows like *Coast to Coast, Midnight Society, Fade to Black,* and many more. He was featured on U.S. Cellular commercials in 2016 and some of them had over four million views. He was on *Destination Fear,* season two, on the Travel Channel featuring the Sheboygan Insane Asylum. His team conducts tours and overnights at some of the most haunted locations in Wisconsin and out of state.

INTRODUCTION

In *Haunted Expeditions in the Midwest*, we take you on a journey to some of the most haunted locations—from blood curdling screams heard throughout the halls of the Sheboygan Insane Asylum in Wisconsin all the way to a final farewell in the middle of Kansas. Embark on a journey with us as we tell you our experiences while investigating firsthand in these haunted locations. We will share with you the history of the location along with any ghost stories from the past. Many emotions go into every investigation that we do as a team, from excitement, to fear, happiness, loneliness, and joy. Every location that we investigate holds an energy and a story to go with it.

In this book the terms *ghost* and *spirit* are used interchangeably; however, in some beliefs the term *ghost* is referred to as someone still on earth and the term *spirit* is someone who has passed over to heaven or another realm and is able to come back at free will. A ghost can appear in a form and likes to haunt people and can sometimes be mischievous. A spirit appears in a misty form otherwise known as an apparition and is not there to haunt someone but to watch over things.

Our investigations are real and never faked and all our evidence is legitimate. We take what we do very seriously and we do not believe in provoking those who have passed. The paranormal world is the world of the unknown; therefore there are no experts in this field, but there are those like us who have a passion for the paranormal. We search for answers to the afterlife with the hope of finding peace for those who are still mourning. We have found through our investigations that many who have passed on really do want to communicate with us. We would like to thank all our followers, friends, and family for all the support over the years. As we always say, "Never pass up an adventure!"

CHAPTER 1

FARRAR SCHOOL
FARRAR, IOWA
By Craig Nehring

Farrar

Farrar is a place that we have investigated more times than I can count. We do yearly events for the public to come and investigate with us. It's about a six-hour drive from us but worth the travel time as we have never been disappointed and always have activity going

1

on in the school. On the drive you will see cornfield after cornfield and then you turn on the road to Farrar and you still see cornfields and you think how in the world is there a school out here. You see a bunch of trees and then a little clearing and in that clearing you find the large school sitting a top a little hill a few yards from a cemetery and not far away is a church. Tons of tall trees surround the school on the sides and in the back. There is a farm next to the school and horses sit watching the team as they enter the school. There is an outside play area that has seemed to have succumbed to old age with even the monkey bars tilted to one side. All that remains is a swing set still upright where kids once swung back and forth on recess. We have been through many storms here that you can see coming across the fields, yet the school has adapted well to the storms over the years and stood the test of time. A sign at the end of the long gravel driveway says Farrar and Maxwell Iowa.

When you start driving up the driveway, the school gets bigger and bigger and in some of the windows you can almost see kids looking out the window waiting for their parents to come and pick them up after school and maybe the ghosts of the children are doing just that. We get out of the car and Jim the owner comes out to meet us and has all the times before. We are ready for two nights of investigations here and guests will arrive tomorrow. We are there a day early to get the school prepared. We walked through the same front doors where so many kids have walked through when it was a functioning school; on the first day of opening the school, a band played and on the very last day when the school was closed forever, the band played once more. My team and I am drawn to this school and for some reason the ghosts of the children past call out to us and most we know by name.

Walking though the front door, you are greeted by a staircase leading to the second floor and the staircase splits two hallways that lead to the first floor. The first floor is where the owners live—an area that's quite small yet cozy. There is a kitchen that is under construction with a dumbwaiter that goes to down to the gym. The kitchen once done will make the school even nicer and be able to serve food maybe for some future events. Two more staircases go up on both ends of the school to reach the top and final floors. Just before you head up, there is a base camp room where most teams reside. There is a small refrigerator and microwave for teams to make some small meals. We have slept in there many times, sometimes on the two couches or the La-Z-Boy chair that they have in there; if there is not enough room, we set up cots and air mattresses to sleep on. There is a bulletin board in the room that has tons of business cards from teams that have been there investigating. Some of the more well-known faces that have been there include Chad Lindberg from *Fast N Furious* and *Ghost Stalkers* and Corey Taylor, the lead singer for Stone Sour. *Kindred Spirits*, the TV show, was also there. We have hosted events with people like Johnny Houser, Richard Estep, and many more.

The second floor has many classrooms to choose from to investigate in and each classroom has a chalkboard on which teams write their names to say they were at the school. One of the rooms on the second floor is the library and I call it the bowling-pin room since there are always bowling - pins in that room. That room is a highly active room with lots of disembodied voices. The rest of the rooms have activity as well and each room presents with a different type of activity. In one of the rooms I had left a voice recorder, which, as we slept, captured a little girl singing, "He loves me, he loves me not." On the second floor you will find two more staircases that lead to the top floor, which is my favorite floor. The auditorium is on the top floor and it is a large room with a stage where the kids used to put on plays and concerts for holidays and more. The room is where I like to sleep when it's not cold outside.

I seem to always hear the pitter-patter of kid's feet running in and out of the room while I try to sleep. The auditorium are the most active place in the school in my opinion. Across the hall are a few more classrooms, also highly active places. There is one more small flight of stairs that goes up to the principal's office, where one of the ghosts reside. He is not the nicest of ghosts there and he likes to mess with the guests. I had an instance of being choked in the base camp area and one of our investigators had a dark shadow hovering over her when she was trying to sleep. She tried to move but she said it felt like the shadow was holding her down. She never investigated with us again after that episode. There is a small room off the principal's office that likely had filing cabinets and other records in it. In that room there is a hole in the ceiling where a ladder was once attached; they went up the ladder to raise the flag on the pole. A medium on an event said that the principal put students up there to discipline them. I don't really think that was the case and never heard any former students say anything like that. While I have heard of some not so nice things happening there, I don't think that had happened and I hope not.

The last floor I am going to talk about is the basement; the basement holds the gym with the basketball court, which held many tournaments in the past when the school was open. There are bathrooms down there for guests and us to use. The bathrooms on the upper floors are no longer in use. I checked one out one time and started singing smoking in the boy's room but was interrupted by a loud scream of a girl I couldn't see. It's possible she didn't like my singing, or I was in the girls' room so that might be part of it too. One side of the gym has a door and that leads to the boiler room. The boiler room is also regularly active, and we have heard things like metal scraping along the floor, and I have been scratched down there as well. Now onto some history.

The History of Farrar

In 1919, C.G. Geddes donated six acres of his farm to merge the area's one-room country schoolhouses. The school boards voted and created the Washington Township Consolidated School District. The cornerstone inscribed with the year 1921 was set and the dedication ceremony commenced on April 1, 1922. The schoolhouse filled with citizens from miles around. An orchestra played on stage in the auditorium as a banquet served the hundreds in attendance. Not all citizens were behind the new building with its $100,000 price tag. One disgruntled citizen refused to attend the celebration calling it a "monument to the arrogance and vanity of the school board," with its boiler heating, electric lights, and indoor bathroom facilities. On May 3, 2002, once again, the band played, a banquet served the hundreds in attendance and sadly, the eighty-year-old schoolhouse closed its doors for the last time.

After sitting abandoned for five years, Jim and Nancy Oliver purchased the building in 2006. It quickly became apparent they were not alone. Voices, shadow people, and orbs were common. Nancy became unsteady on the stairs when a hand on her shoulder helped her catch her balance. She turned to thank her husband for the help only to find no one there. The dark distinct outline of a small boy was sighted on the well-lit stairway descending into the gymnasium. The boy appeared to be about three feet, six inches tall with one foot on each step and holding onto the handrail. The figure stayed motionless for almost two seconds before disappearing . . .

The large 17,000 square foot schoolhouse looks out of place in the small town of Farrar. Farrar's population of no more than thirty people has been slowly shrinking for many years. The only growing population is in the 150-year-old cemetery across from the schoolhouse.

The Investigations of Farrar

This past year of 2021, we investigated for three nights with one of the nights without guests. This was more of a relaxing investigation, just getting everything ready for the guests. It was rather warm out, so we spent most of the evening before dark outside where it was slightly less stuffy. One of our helpers thought it would be cool to impress the girls by breathing fire, which backfired and burned his neck in the process. If I had known that he was going to become a human roman candle I would have told him no but I wasn't around when he attempted it. After he attended to the his burns, we were ready to start the investigation. We headed to the auditorium to see if anyone wanted to talk. We were not up there long when we got some audio on the voice recorder that showed up saying "They're back" and "He missed us," which was referring to me since I am there all the time and they know who we are.

We now concentrated on the stage area, asking questions to see if they would make some noise. We started hearing footsteps on the stage but could not see anything visible. I, along with one other investigator, saw a large shadow move from a doorway close the stage and then move back though the same door. We believe this was the principal named Mike that is described as the dark shadow figure that roams the halls in search of students who are not in class. We kept hearing footsteps and loud knocks by the stage and even some stuff coming from out in the hallway, almost like they were scared to come in the room and join us.

During our past investigations, we had seen that same shadow come into the room and leave but we had also seen a little girl standing by the stage area; she liked to play with the meters we had on the floor by lighting them up to tell us she was with us. I always buy a toy and bring it to the school so the kids have something different to play with. One of our first investigations at the school we heard all this racket in the walls that was downright scary, and we had no idea what it was. Later, while sitting down in the base room we were watching the video on the cameras we had set up and saw six sets of red eyes. There were raccoons in the walls and that was the noise but found a hole where they had gotten out and were walking around the school. They are no longer there and the access they had to get in is no longer available. We once had an investigator with an air mattress, and he set that up close to the door where we see the shadow figures. While he was lying on that mattress, something of the unseen nature ran into the room running across the air mattress making it jump up into the air and him yelling out saying, "What the hell was that?." I had video recording running that night and on replay of the video during that event we could clearly see an apparition run into and back out of the room. I sat by the stage after that had happened with my back against the stage when a loud knock made me jump. It was right behind me; there is an access panel inside the stage to go underneath and I wonder if something wanted to come out. I sat there awhile longer and yelled Marco and on the voice recorder something could be heard yelling "polo" back to me. I like the ghosts at Farrar since they all seem to have a sense of humor but then again, they were kids that likely enjoyed playing tricks.

The case of the disappearing flashlight on the stage was also from an early investigation of the school. We set a mag light on the stage but forgot it was there. We went to grab it in the morning, but it was gone. Where did it go? We didn't think any other investigators had picked it up so we thought we would go over video to check to see who picked it up. What we found put us in state of shock. The flashlight was there and literally just was seen disappearing into thin air in front of the video camera and never to be found the rest of the trip, almost like it was sucked into a different dimension. The owners would tell us in the weeks to follow that people who drove by would see someone holding a flashlight in the upper windows, yet no one was in the school.

The auditorium in the school

Our next stop for the investigation was the gym close to the boiler room, where during investigations in the past we have head basketball games going on early in the morning only to find out it's pitch black and no one is there. This time however one of the lockers close to the girls' bathroom slammed shut and things were heard being tossed at us while we sat in the dark. On audio I captured a voice that says, "Help me" and "Kitten." I hear ghost say help me quite a bit on most of the locations that I go. We sat there for a while and heard a loud noise come from the base camp room on the other side of the wall, but no one was in there.

The gym

The morning was closing in fast and we knew we should get some sleep so that we could stay up with the guests and investigate since they were showing up at 3:00 p.m. and we still needed to get quite a bit ready. We called it a night even though some still stayed up; most of us headed to bed.

Guest night was here, and we had everyone staying in the gym since it's closest to the bathrooms so they don't have to navigate the stairs in the dark. The gym is also much cooler on hot summer days. The first stop was the library to investigate but I call it the pins room. We settled into the room and, once everyone was quiet, started to ask questions. One of the guests was touched by something in the room and it pulled their hair a couple of times. I checked audio on my voice recorder, and I heard something I hadn't heard since the first time we investigated the school. We heard a male voice say "Lucas." It had been so long since I heard the same person talking about Lucas. The first recording I ever heard there said "Lucas can't see me." It was the same voice and the same person talking about Lucas so it was amazing to know some of the same ghosts were there from many years ago. This wouldn't be the last time I was amazed this weekend by something from the past. One prior event from the library on an investigation many years ago happened when one of our investigators was hugged by an unseen source and she felt the arms wrap around her. She was so scared that she had to leave the area. She went back to base camp and never left that room during the rest of the investigation.

Next stop was a room that sits across from the auditorium and a room where in the past I had heard a little girl singing a song with the words, "He loves me, he loves me not." I also heard a growl and felt a huge draft in this room. We decided to take the guests in this room and try it out.

Head of the class

We heard some noises in the room and things in the hallway walking around but not too much was happening, so we decided to take a break and grab a late-night snack from the cooler. I forgot I left the voice recorder up in the room, which was normally fine when I was sleeping but I needed it for the rest of the night. I headed back up there to grab it and brought it back down to base where I was; we were eating while everyone else was on a break.

I decided to check the audio and to my surprise saw a blimp in the audio showing something had been recorded. I listened and there it was the little girl that I had heard singing in the school before. This time she was singing something else, but it was hard to make out what it was. I was surprised it was the same voice again, proving that the same ghosts are still hanging at Farrar and are likely there every time we go. We had one more location to visit for the night and I wanted to save the most intense part of the investigation that we had with guests for last.

We decided to hit up one more room that we always seem to have activity in. This room is on the second floor and had a bunch of cylinders with artwork on them from the kids who went to school there. There are chairs and a desk, and the windows are covered up and seems to be a darker room even during the day. There is a cloak room, and we would always hear noises coming from that room. Maybe a kid was stuck in there or put in there on a time-out, but for some reason tonight it seemed like a darker energy was with us in there. Our guest sat in the desks and I sat at the teacher's desk while another investigator sat in the cloak room. I started to use the ghost box and there was a very deep voice coming out of it and saying things like "demon" and "evil", which is sometimes normal as they like to say things you don't want to hear. The deep voice was still talking, and I decided to let the box run. I got up to do some video taping in the room and was pointing it back toward the cloak room when suddenly a shadow moved from within the room; none of us saw it dart into the cloak room, but our investigator jumped up and out of there as he felt it brush past him and a breeze followed. The guests were a little on edge but that was why they were here, and they wanted to see and hear stuff that now was a reality. Whatever was in the room was still there hiding among us, but we no longer saw the shadow as it disappeared into thin air. There was a heaviness to the room, and I could feel that something was still there.

The cloak room of the classroom

I decided to put the camera down and sit in the cloak room myself and see if anything would happen while I was in there. The other investigator felt better that I was there and decided to come back and join me on one side while another guest sat on the other side of me. We all sat in the dark with just a little light coming through a window from an outside light. It was quiet when suddenly I heard a footstep next to me, but no one moved so it was what was in the room with us. It grabbed the guest, who got up quickly and left the area. I didn't feel anything but was waiting for it to touch me, but it didn't. There were only two of us now in the small cloak room and some of the other guests heard noises in the back of the classroom by the chalk-board. We all thought we heard a scream come from somewhere in the distance or maybe out in the hallway. I stood up and asked the ghost if we were making him mad when suddenly out in the hallway the lockers all slammed shut one right after the other. I ran to the door and looked around at the lockers and they were all closed but now were opening slowly, which they do on their own, but they don't close on their own, so someone used some force to slam them back into the frame. I saw nothing in the hallway. I thought I heard foot-steps in the distance walking my way and decided to retreat into the room and sit back down to see if whatever was responsible for the disturbance in the hall would come back in and join us.

The lockers in the hallway

Now back in the room, I waited in the cloakroom for more things to happen. One other person was still in there with me. One of the guests said something just went past her in my direction. I heard another loud footstep and something run right past me and I felt the breeze. It wasn't there to mess with me but to grab my other investigator; it was odd that it was not bothering me at all but going after the others. My other investigator said he was done and decided to leave the area and the guests said we need a break, which was fine with me.

We have events here every year for guests and hope to see new faces each year and like always want to thank Jim and Nancy Oliver, the owners of the school, for years of fun at this location.

CHAPTER 2

SHAKER'S CIGAR BAR
MILWAUKEE, WISCONSIN
By Melissa Clevenger

Shaker's Bar

When I think of haunted bars in Wisconsin that I would like to investigate, the first one that comes to my mind is Shaker's Bar. In

February 2021, we got the call we had been waiting for, and we were invited to Shaker's Bar to take part in a podcast for their YouTube channel, along with a full tour, investigation of the place, and finally an overnight stay in the third-floor penthouse. At this point I honestly did not know any of the history of the bar; I just knew that it was very well known for being haunted and that I could not wait to go and experience this place. Knowing at one point that Al Capone owned the building spiked my interest even more.

Our overnight investigation of Shaker's Cigar Bar included me, Craig, Travis, and Savanah. As we drove by the bar, I could not help but notice the beauty of the building. Purple lights illuminated the building and made the bar look so welcoming. Once we finally found a decent parking spot, the four of us began our short walk to the entrance of the bar. We just happened to pick the coldest day so far this year and by morning it was 28 degrees below zero with the windshield! We were frozen by the time we got to the door. After a few short moments to unthaw, we were finally able to take in the atmosphere.

Since the bar was open for its regular hours, I was a little worried about the smoke since it was in fact a cigar bar. Surprisingly even with patrons smoking cigars the bar did not seem smokey at all, which was a pleasant surprise. We were immediately greeted by our host, Leah, who began to take us to our table. Before we could take our seats, Bob, the owner of Shaker's, greeted us with a smile and a handshake as he led us to the back corner where we would film live for their YouTube channel. This was a great time to sit and chat and hear stories directly from Bob and for him to get to know us and our history as a team. After hearing some of his stories about the bar, I was even more excited to begin our investigation.

Once we were finished filming for the podcast, we headed to a table where we could eat dinner while we waited for our 10 o'clock tour of the building. The food was great, and it gave us a little more time to take in the atmosphere around us. From what we experienced I can honestly say that Bob runs a great establishment; although we came for the ghost that haunt the place, we were thoroughly impressed.

The History of Shaker's Cigar Bar

The building that would later become known as Shaker's Cigar Bar was constructed in 1894. It originally opened as a Schlitz Brewery cooperage house where they would make huge barrels for brewing beer and transport. Through the years the building was sold several times. In 1905, it was used as a distribution center. In 1924, it changed hands once again to be opened as a speakeasy. This is where the history gets interesting.

Brothers Al and Frank Capone opened the speakeasy as a soda-bottling operation. The soda-bottling operation served as a cover for the liquor that was being consumed and produced on site. The front entry remained locked and the entrance to the speakeasy was through the entrance in the alleyway. The second and third floor of the building were used as a brothel. The second floor was for what were known as the B girls. There was a fluff room where the receptionist would get the clients ready for their girl. This floor was more of an in-and-out operation where you would pay for the services that you wanted to receive. Also located on the second floor was what was known as the abortion room. In this room a doctor on site would check for STDs and perform abortions for the girls. This history is not so pleasant. Times were quite different then, but it is just that, a part of our history. The A girl would reside on the third floor where she would have her own sponsor. Her life was a little better than the B girls although her life was still not considered easy.

As with any place owned by mobsters Al and Frank Capone, there are endless stories of punishments and murder. The speakeasy continued operation into the 1940s. In 1986, owner Bob Weiss opened Shaker's Cigar Bar. Shaker's Cigar Bar is in Milwaukee's Third Ward and as a cigar bar it is the only place you can legally smoke inside in the entire city of Milwaukee. Inside you will find a beautiful Victorian-style bar and the atmosphere almost brings you back to times of the past. Almost everything inside is not original to the building but dates to the time of original operation. Some of these articles are said to have brought a few new ghosts with them.

During renovations in 2001, they found human remains inside one of the walls. Those remains were said to be that of a woman's and the bones dated back seventy years. They also were able to use equipment to see below the cement floors in the basement where they found numerous bones, which also dated back over seventy years. Most of the bones were fragments and separated, but in the far-right corner of the basement two full skeletons were discovered side by side.

Fake skeletons reside in place of real ones

In the later years there are stories of Jeffrey Dahmer frequenting the bar. This was before anyone knew what he did behind the scenes. Many high-class residents and police captains were known to go to the bar, and it is believed that Dahmer got a kick out of standing next to them and they had no idea about the murders that he had committed. Shaker's Cigar Bar offers many ghost tours for the public to go on and they have now added the Jeffrey Dahmer tour as well. So much history in one building.

The Investigation of the Shaker's Cigar Bar

We were now ready for our tour of the building, and luckily it was only four of us for the tour. Leah was our tour guide, and she was amazing, very smart and maybe a little spunky, which made for a great tour. To begin we headed down to the basement, which had a very eerie feeling. Knowing that Al Capone was a former owner, you can only imagine the horror that took place in that very basement along with what or who could possibly be buried underneath the cement that we were standing on. During our tour Leah gave us history along with stories of paranormal things that have happened in the building. We were able to investigate each area along the way, and Bob joined us on our investigations when he was able to get away from the bar area.

As we stood there in the basement with all of us wearing our facemasks, I couldn't help but wonder if this past year and a half has been just as hard on the spirits as it has been on us. It is a vastly different world we live in right now, and I question if it even phases the spirits. Do the spirits sense or know the hardships that we have been going through? Do they understand why we are standing there wearing masks or do they even care? I am sure the energy of the living around them was different from the energy a year and a half ago. Investigating, even with a mask on, gives me even just for a moment a sense of normalcy that we have missed for so long.

We began to descend toward the back of the basement when we came across an old safe that they said they found in the basement when Bob purchased the building. Unfortunately to this day they have been unable to unlock the safe to see what or who is locked up inside. My mind instantly went to the story of the sword and the stone, so I had to see for myself if maybe I was the lucky one. After a couple of attempts, I accepted my defeat and decided that the safe was not meant to be opened. We began to walk a little further back into the basement when Craig began to feel violently ill and he instantly had to sit down. His skin was pale and clammy while his head was pounding, and his stomach began to hurt. After a few minutes of this he decided that he needed to head upstairs to lie down while we finished the tour. Leah suggested that I use the dowsing rods that they had down there to begin to ask some questions of the ghosts that were down there. About five minutes later Craig comes walking back down the stairs toward us. After how violently sick he was, the moment he got out of the basement he felt completely fine. Now we had to wonder if it was something in the basement that made him feel that way.

The safe in the basement

I continued to ask several questions with the dowsing rods and seemed to be getting good responses with them. Then suddenly Craig yells out that he felt like something had just stabbed him in the lower back. He was in quite a bit of pain and nothing was around him that could have stabbed him. At this point we determined that there must be a spirit in the basement that did not want Craig down there for some reason. After a little longer in the basement we decided to continue our tour and investigation on another floor to give Craig a little break from the malicious spirit that was after him.

The second and third floor used to be a brothel. We walked through the second floor but then headed up to the third-floor penthouse where we would be staying. This was the floor that the A girl would stay. This girl would have her own sponsor and would occupy the entire third floor.

The penthouse was the entire third floor of the building. There was a bathroom with a ceramic bathtub, a full kitchen, a sitting room, a living room, and a bedroom with a wood-burning fireplace. They told stories of a girl named Molly, who at about the age of sixteen had ran away from home only to begin working at the speakeasy. She began her career on the second floor in the fluff room because of her young age, but in time she got a sponsor and became the A girl on the third floor. An old childhood friend named Pat found her there one day and continually tried to talk Molly into leaving with him. Molly, however, was happy with her life at the brothel and refused to leave yet she still would see Pat and talk to him. One day Molly was with her sponsor when Pat paid the security guard a large amount of money to let him have some time with Molly. Upon arriving upstairs Pat soon realizes that Molly's sponsor was in fact his own father. In a fit of rage Pat murders Molly once his dad leaves and according to the story it wasn't long after that Pat also vanished.

Supposedly the spirits that occupy the upstairs are mainly that of Molly and occasionally Pat. Once we began investigating, we soon realized that we were communicating with Pat. We were using the ghost box along with our Mel Meter with REM. In the basement we were getting a few intelligent responses with the ghost box; however upstairs we were only getting static. We then asked if Pat was in the room with us and instantly the Mel Meter began to go off. We continued to ask a variety of questions while we received responses from the Mel Meter. By this time, it was getting late and we were all ready to head to bed and call it a night.

At about 3:30 a.m. Travis headed to go to the bathroom as I reminded him to watch his step when he leaves the bathroom. When you open the bathroom door there is a short step down with no warning. I began to doze back to sleep when I heard a loud boom and realized that Travis must have forgotten about the step coming out of the bathroom. Luckily once I yelled to ask if he was OK, he began to laugh. We then fell back to sleep.

After lying there for about another hour, I began to wonder if anything would happen to us during the night. Just then there was a loud bang that came from the front of the room that Travis and I were in. At the same time Travis and I both jumped up saying "What in the world was that!" Well, that would not be the only time that night that Travis and I said that. At about 5:00 a.m. I heard what sounded like the creaking of the gate on the stairway opening all the way. The four of us were the only ones in the building for the night so I knew that nobody else was in the building. Probably about twenty minutes later I heard a lady's voice coming from the stairway, and Travis heard it as well. We both sat straight up in bed out of a deep sleep and at the same time said, "Did you hear that? That was a ladies voice on the stairway!"

The bed in the room where guests now sleep

Although I did not feel anything throughout the night or see anything, I was happy that we had the experiences that we did. The loud bang, the creaking gate, the ladies voice was all heard by both Travis and me. When we finally woke up in the morning, we asked Craig and Savanah if they heard the lady on the stairway talking last night. They did not, in fact, hear anything that Travis and I had heard. Possibly they were just so tired that they slept through it all or it could be because the room Travis and I slept in was closer to the stairway. It was now time for us to pack up and get ready to head home. I am so glad that we got the opportunity to experience the rich history of Shaker's Cigar Bar for ourselves. It really was a great experience and investigation.

Melissa using dousing rods in the basement

CHAPTER 3

GENERAL ASAHEL STONE MANSION WINCHESTER, INDIANA

By Craig Nehring

General Asahel Stone Mansion

I was looking for a good place to investigate and take some of my friends and a new member on our team to an investigation so she could learn a few new things. The rest of my team wanted to sit things out since they had a busy year, but I am always up for a ghost hunt. I thought about this place because we investigated the Randolph Asylum a few years back and the owners just gaining access to this place as well, plus the owners had another location called the Blackford County Jail, which will be in the next chapter. We decided we would investigate this place the first night and the jail the second night, and we would get to sleep in both places. On our two-night investigation we had Brittnie, Kara, Jason, Drew, Jennifer, Lisa, Danyelle, and myself.

We headed down south toward Indiana, and we were to arrive all pretty close in the same time frame but got there about an hour before we would gain access to the mansion. We decided to take pictures of the outside of the mansion. It was decorated for Halloween since it was October. Unfortunately it was extremely cold outside. I love to take pictures but all I wanted to do was get inside and out of the cold. The women like always were in selfie mode, and one of them brought a selfie stick. I avoided that picture method. This was a large mansion that needed a new paint job. There were endless windows all around the mansion and the top floor had windows that seemed to be set out from the house, which I found odd but would find out later what that was all about. We walked around the place and took a bunch of pictures; when we got back to the front there was our host waiting to give us a tour, so we headed inside the mansion.

Once inside it was quite a bit warmer, and I was under the impression the whole place was heated but that wasn't the case. It was only one main room that was heated even though they had wall furnaces on most floors in the room, but none were turned on. I guess some had issues. The room that was the warmest we would use as the base camp area and the place to sleep when we finally would pass out. Just inside the back door was a staircase going down the stairs and a small kitchen that sat off to the right with a sink and microwave. There was a hallway leading into a few other areas like our base camp room and another room with a grand piano in it. Maybe the ghosts would play for us tonight because I wasn't going to and only know one note. There was a staircase leading to the second floor and a bunch of bedrooms. I picked one of the rooms to set up. Since claims of activity seemed to happen more on the second floor, I thought it would be cool to sleep there as well. The host said if you look out that window across the street you will see four houses that look the same. That was true indeed. She said while the house was being built Asahel built the houses for his workers so they could be close to the mansion since they were the ones building it. That was a nice gesture to build houses for his workers and their families to live in so they didn't have to travel. I guess it would be hard to say to your boss sorry I can't come to work today I live too far away or if they called in sick, he could check on them to see if they were OK. The staircase that we had come up was all wooden stairs, no carpet. I figured we would hear someone coming up them like others had said that they would hear phantom footsteps in the night. We continued the tour, which headed up one more level to the star-gazing room as the General loved to look at the stars and this is where I learned why the windows stuck out from the house. He had them built that way on purpose so he could tilt in and look up at the sky so the eaves of the house would not block the view. I looked up and saw a skeleton friend on the weather vane, which made me jump as I didn't expect to see anything outside the window. There were a few smaller rooms off the star-gazing room, and they needed some repairs. Old-fashioned wallpaper that even the craziest of people would not have in their house today was peeling away from the walls and the carpet in these rooms reminded me of my Grandma's house when I was little. I smelled something rotten but quickly noted that the wall furnace had a little gas leak; however it was nothing that would make us go boom. Our last stop would be the basement, which looked like any other basement, but I guess I thought it would be bigger. It had a few small rooms but nothing that really creeped me out at all. The house looked creepy on the outside but the inside really wasn't that bad. I did notice that almost every room in the house had an ivory fireplace and would also find out more about that when we went over the history. The host left us the keys to the mansion and headed out, and we unpacked our cars and gear and set everything up in the base camp room waiting on darkness to fall upon us. I noticed it was getting much colder and the temperature would fall below freezing point tonight. I thought of investigating the warm room all night.

The History of the Mansion

General Asahel Stone Mansion was constructed in 1872 in Winchester, Indiana.

General Stone Mansion is built in the architectural style known as Second Empire. Prior to construction, a series of catalog style houses were built east of the site, which remain. These were built to house the construction crew and their loved ones during the Stone Mansion construction.

All the marble fireplaces are made of imported Carrara marble, the quarry Michelangelo got all his marble from. The Stone Mansion was built for Asahel Stone and his wife, Lydia, who never had any children. He had a long list of accomplishments.

Asahel Stone was born June 29, 1817 in Marietta, Ohio, and he was the son of Ezra Stone, who was a carpenter and contractor.

Asahel Stone was a state senator before and after the Civil War. He was instrumental in shifting the railroad to come through Winchester and his own property. Asahel Stone was commissary general and state quarter master general during the Civil War.

He oversaw the State Bakery, which provided for government-run institutions including the military hospitals and prisons, as well as veteran, widow, and orphan homes.

Asahel Stone was the president, a director, and a stockholder of the Randolph Co. Bank (1879).

Asahel Stone donated forty acres to establish the Fountain Park Cemetery as a public cemetery for the citizens of Winchester, Indiana, on March 1, 1880.

At the time, you would be able to see his burial plot from the master bedroom.

Asahel Stone died on February 25, 1891, in Winchester, Indiana.

Other interesting notes: The general was a star gazer and built the third floor with windows that extend beyond the house to allow a clear view of the night sky. The general was only five feet tall.

Asahel Stone willed the Stone Mansion to Lydia upon his death. Lydia Stone died on September 18, 1892.

The mansion now is owned by a nonprofit organization called Save the Old Properties.

General Asahel

The ivory fireplaces

The Investigation

It was finally dark, and we could start our investigation. Our first stop was the basement, and we all congregated in one of the bigger rooms and spread out. We started asking questions and waiting for noises while remaining silent. Someone saw a flash of light but that was quickly debunked by the car lights on the window of the basement as the road lined up with the window. We thought we heard a voice but were apprehensive about it being from the inside of the mansion. The next night was Halloween, so kids were running around outside more than usual. I turned on the ghost box to see if anyone wanted to communicate but picked up nothing but static and no voices. I did however pick up a voice on the recorder of a ghost saying his name was Tom. We went from room to room with no luck, so we headed up to the main floor and tried some more stuff there but to no avail. I said we should try the second floor with all the bedrooms. It was much colder up there, and we had to bundle up, and there was no way in heck I was sleeping where I couldn't feel my nose. We all sat quietly, and then it started with the footsteps coming up the stairs. I walked over to look; no one was there but I could hear them, clunk, clunk, clunk and even the banister shook. I stepped back from the stairs as the footsteps were getting closer to the top and didn't want anything to toss me over the banister. Kara was standing at the top now in front of me, and she felt something touch her and push off to the side like the ghost needed to get through. I thought they could go right through you, but I guess this ghost hadn't learned that yet.

I was now down the hall and looking toward the staircase while others were in the other bedrooms. I had a REM pod, a device that has an antenna coming out of it so that if something touches it the device will light up with different colors for intensity. That device was just down from the stairs. I thought I heard a voice followed by the REM pod going off and a loud crashing that sounded like the bathtub just fell though the floor into the living room below.

That was followed by some of the girls on our team screaming. I asked what had happened. The ivory of one of the fireplaces gave way from the wall and crashed down onto the floor of one of the bedrooms. On closer inspection one could see the deterioration of the mortar that kept it in place, which explained why it fell. What it didn't explain was the scream I heard just seconds before the crash and the REM pod going off. Was one of the ghosts trying to warn us this was about to happen? We decided to stay up there and continue since it seemed like with the footsteps, we would get more activity. I asked some more questions and tried the shave and a haircut on the wall next to me to see if something would knock back. The first try ended with the exact timing of someone slamming the door of a car outside and the second time a dog barked twice. We thought that was crazy but still not paranormal; it was funny to say the least. I needed to try it one more time and knocked a couple of times to try to get a response. This time two knocks were heard inside the mansion by the staircase followed by a loud voice that a few of us heard; we think it said "Stop."

I listened back to the audio and caught some voices saying stuff to us. A girl's voice said "Mallory" and a male voice said "Go touch them." I didn't feel like I got touched but a few others did. Things started to quiet down now but we wanted to take a quick peek in the star-gazing area in case someone was up there. We went up to the top level. It was very cold up there, and we were all going to need a break soon to warm up. On the very top floor, I heard a faint whisper, and someone said "Go slap him." Nothing happened that we were aware of unless this was residual, and the ghost was talking about slapping someone else many years ago. It again became incredibly quiet, so we decided to head down to the first floor and get warm by the heater before heading back out for round two. The warmth of the base camp area made us never want to leave that room again since the rest of the house was an icebox.

Our base camp area in the mansion

We were warm now and dreaded going back out in the cold and I was tired from the long drive but wanted to go out one last time and investigate. We braved the cold as we headed back to the second floor one last time to see if we could communicate with what we heard before. We stayed in the same areas and thought we heard a scream again come from within the mansion somewhere and indeed we did as it was picked up on audio but that would be the last thing we would hear that night. It was so quiet that you could hear a pin drop. I was thinking maybe the ghosts are as cold as I am and some of the team was shivering in the corners trying to stay warm. I said I have some good footage and audio to go over and am content in going to sleep since we still had one more place to visit the next night. I told the rest of the team to feel free to stay up and investigate, and some did for about an hour after me but even they had enough of the cold and retreated to the heated room. Even with the heated room, the cold outside was too much for the small heater on the wall. I noticed Brittnie slept with her winter coat on all night. I still couldn't feel my nose when I woke up. We would like to come back when its warmer and hang with the ghosts when they are not cold too.

CHAPTER 4

PRESTON RESIDENTS FAREWELL MARQUETTE, KANSAS

By Melissa Clevenger

The Preston Residence

This chapter is about my childhood home that I grew up in and spent most of my life. A home that holds so many wonderful memories for me, as well as a lifetime of haunted memories. Where do I even start? I think the most fitting way to start this chapter is with a poem that I wrote.

Missing Pieces

I am not whole
For with each loss that I have lived through
A piece of me has broken off.
Yet with all the loss, I am not fragile
I have grown to who I am today because of you
And yet I am forever in search of you
A glimpse of your smile,
a fragment of your voice
If only I could make your memories come alive.

I think of my life in some ways like a puzzle. My life started off as a million pieces in a box with no picture to it. Slowly through the years, each piece of the puzzle began to get color, until finally the puzzle seemed to be a complete picture of me. Every person that I have met along the way played a part in how my puzzle looked. Weather it was a beautiful bright piece or a dark piece, they were all important.

And then the day comes where a piece of the puzzle is lost, and you cannot find it anywhere no matter how hard you search. You will always remember what that puzzle piece looked like, and what an important part it played in the puzzle, but it is forever gone and is now a hole. That is how I think of death. Each person in my life played an important part of who I am today, and when they pass away, I lose a part of myself; it creates a hole in my heart. That is why we are so thankful for memories, because our memories help to fill those holes in. And although they are gone, they will always be a part of me. Just like the missing puzzle piece, I have forever been in search of proof of life after death.

My investigations often bring peace to me just knowing that our loved ones are still with us every day. I believe they can be anywhere at any time; we just need to slow down a little and pay attention. Sometimes we get so caught up in what or who we have lost that we forget to cherish every moment with those who are still with us. Just remember that they will always be a part of you.

The History of the Preston Residence

Marquette, Kansas, is a small farming town that was named after Marquette, Michigan. In 1873, Marquette began with a flourmill that was located on the banks of the Smoky Hill River. The downtown area of Marquette has a historical feel to it with Victorian-style buildings that are listed on the Kansas State Register of Historic Places.

The parents of Howard and Kermit Peterson built what would later become the Preston Residence in the early months of 1905. Howard and Cecil Peterson lived in the house and were the owners of the grocery store across the alley. In the backyard there was an underground freezer for storing food. Cecil was a dentist, but he never pursued his career. Then in May 1905 a devastating tornado ripped through the town leveling almost the entire community. Very few houses survived the tornado; however, the Petersons' house still stood.

In 1977, Larry and Brenda Preston purchased the house along with their new son Eric. The house was perfect for the new family, with nine rooms and five bedrooms, and Marquette was the perfect little town to raise kids in. The family was complete in June 1979 with the birth of their daughter Melissa. The room that would become my room was completely full of dental equipment from the previous owners.

The haunted history of the Preston Residence began with me when I was incredibly young. The first memory that I have was when I was about five years old. We kept all our shoes at the end of the hallway right before the stairs. My mom sent me to go get my shoes from the hallway, which was always scary for me as a child. As I approached the banister, I peered up to the top of the stairs and sitting on the railing at the very top was Jesus' mom, Mary. I do not know how I knew it was Mary sitting there but trust me I knew. She was beautiful and she just sat there silently, and then she gave me the sweetest, purest smile you could ever imagine. I froze for a couple of minutes and could only stare back at her. Then the terror took over my body and I bolted down the hallway back to where my mom stood. I never told my parents about this experience, but I do believe that Mary gave me my gift of being able to see and hear spirits. This would be one of my first of many experiences in this house.

I could write an entire book on my experiences in my house growing up, but with only having a chapter I will let you hear my most memorable stories. It was quite common for me to see ghosts in my house; in fact, it was daily. The ghost did not always interact with me; for the most part it was like they did not even see me. On several occasions I saw two ghosts walk past my bedroom door, and they looked like they were just walking and talking to each other. They never even bothered to look at me. That is the thing with this house; there was no shortage of spirits and they carried on as if they were just passing through.

One night when I was about nine years old, a young boy, probably around ten years old, rose from the side of my bed. He had an antique look to him. The boy was lying flat with his arms to his side and he was looking straight up. His body rose from the side of my bed closest to the closet, and he rose all the way up and through the ceiling. Another night I was facing my closet, and there was an old, scary man lying in the bed next to me. The man was at least eighty years old, and I could tell he was a ghost although he looked human. I hid under my covers and was terrified. Several scarier things would happen in the years to come from between my bed and the closet. From that point forward I never faced the closet when I went to bed or when I slept.

Anytime I would have sleepovers at my house with friends something would usually happen to scare us. We often would sneak out late in the night to go play in the local park. On one night my brother and I and two other friends were creeping across the living room to sneak out when we heard my mom Brenda yell at us to get back to bed. All four of us turned to face my mom and saw her standing right behind us. Before we could answer her, she faded away. This was not the first time that my mom appeared to us or yelled at us only to disappear.

One morning I heard my mom yell from her bedroom at me to get the cat out of the laundry basket. There was a laundry basket full of clothes in the hallway, but no cat in it. I walked into my mother's bedroom to tell her and she was not there. I then went into the bathroom to take a shower, and after a few minutes in there the shower door flew open and slammed back shut. This was when I realized that I was all alone in the house. Activity typically would be very severe when I was home alone. When others where in the house with me the ghosts were all around but would pretty much keep to themselves. When they knew that I was alone, however, doors would slam and voices were loud.

Fast forward to April 30, 1997. I remember every detail of that day as if it were yesterday. My parents had gotten a divorce, so my mom lived in Wisconsin at this time. My brother and I had scheduled nights to talk to my mom on the phone. This night was not one of the scheduled nights, but for some reason my brother and I had to call my mom so we could each talk to her. After hanging up, my brother went to his girlfriend's house for about an hour. That night I was excited to watch The Ellen DeGeneres show; it was her coming out episode which was unheard of in those days. Right before the show was to begin, I went to walk into the kitchen. When I got to the doorway my brother Eric was just standing there. He looked like a ghost, and I never heard him come in the door. I told him he scared me, but I will never forget how he looked like a ghost. My brother then watched the entire show with me, which was a rare occasion.

May 1, 1997. Yet another day I will never forget. I remember getting ready for school and walking in the kitchen to see a note on the table. My brother needed my dad to go to the bank and make his truck payment for him. My school day was typical until I got to

Government class. I sat at my desk and I just knew that something was wrong. I stood up and sat down probably twenty times. I did not know what to do. I knew something was wrong and I needed to call home, but I did not know what to tell my teacher.

Finally, it was the end of the school day. As I got onto the school bus, my horrible feeling continued to get even worse. By this time, I felt that I was probably going to die on my way home. I honestly thought that somehow, I was going to die. As I walked up to my house, I saw people there and I just knew something was terribly wrong. I walked in the house and my dad took me into the dining room and told me to sit in the wooden rocking chair because he had something that he needed to tell me. This was the moment my life would change and would never be the same.

My brother Eric worked for a construction company. He was placing flags along the road to create the path for the new road. As he was placing the flags, a guy in an earth mover was coming from behind. For some reason that we may never know, the guy decided to turn the machine and drive away. Nobody even realized what happened; they kept working. Somebody then realized my brother was lying in the mud face down. I lost my only brother, Eric, on May 1, 1997.

Eric Wayne Preston November 23, 1976-May 1, 1997

This is the story that I knew of for nearly twenty years. Upon investigating my dad's house last year my brother gave me the answers that I needed to hear. During a ghost box session, I asked several questions; however, I did not hear any responses at the time of the investigation. On my way back to Wisconsin, I went over all my audio from the investigation, and what I heard was astonishing. My brothers voice said that he lived in the house with me, him and our dad and he said Preston. This verified that it was him. He then said, "Sorry that I died. Eric messed up." The importance of this is that I blamed the guy who ran him over for twenty years.

What he meant by Eric messed up was that when the earth movers had stopped, he ran to the front of them to clean off the blades, which was also one of his jobs. Eric had thought that the driver saw him cleaning the blade, so he didn't tell him he was doing it. The driver unfortunately did not even know that Eric was there, so he drove on leaving my brother face down in the mud. So, after twenty years of blaming someone for his death, an investigation of my dad's house and an answer from my brother Eric was what I needed to finally forgive.

After my brother died and before the funeral, several family members were coming from out of state. I was upset because I needed to get clean sheets for everyone, and I could not find any. My brother's door had a latch lock at the very top of the door. As I was standing in front of his door upset about the sheets, the lock lifted and unlocked. I decided to look in my brothers' room because there had to be some reason for the door to unlock. Sitting right there clean and folded at the end of his bed was a stack of clean sheets. I never doubted that he was not there.

Shortly after Eric's death, I had a dream about him. In my dream I walked out of my house and walked to the end of the sidewalk. When I looked across the street, I saw my brother walking toward me from the grocery store. He walked up to me as if nothing were wrong. At first, I was so happy to see him and all I could do was hug him. Then I realized that he was not supposed to be alive, so I pushed him away. I asked my brother why he was there because he was not supposed to be alive.

A few weeks later I had another dream about my brother Eric. In this dream I was at the elementary school that we went to as kids. I walked by the library and sitting there was my brother. He looked at me and smiled and waved. He was probably about ten years old in this dream, and he was wearing a baby-blue t-shirt that I remember him wearing when he was younger. I have thought about those dreams many times through the years. I honestly believe that my brother came back to me in a dream as a child because of how I reacted to him when he came to me at the age of his death.

Not long after my brother Eric's death, I went away to college and then a few years later moved to Wisconsin. My dad continued to live in the house, all alone. The reason that this chapter is called "The Preston Residents' Farewell" is because on December 4, 2020, my dad sold our childhood house to some wonderful new owners. As far as a haunted house, I can say that this house is truly haunted.

The Investigation of the Preston Residence

December 4, 2020, would be the final day in the house as I remember it. My husband, Travis, myself, and our boys, Kaleb and Colton, jumped in the truck to head from Wisconsin to Kansas for the week to pack up my dad's house. I knew this would not be an easy feat considering all the memories that those walls held, but I knew that this day would someday come. Much of our trip was spent packing boxes and deciding what to throw away, and after forty-three years in a house believe me there was a lot to throw away.

During one of the days while I was packing up my old bedroom, my childhood friends Keri and Kelly stopped by. We enjoyed reminiscing about old times, and they had some ghost stories to share that they remembered from my house. It is funny how all my friends have ghost stories from my house. Stories that were so scary for a child that they had never forgot them. Piece by piece we packed up each room; it was not emotional at all like I thought it would be.

Keri and Kelly helping me pack

The final room that we packed up was my brother Eric's room. A room that had been frozen in time. Nothing had changed in Eric's room in twenty-three years. The bed was still made from that fateful day, the calendar still hung on the wall showing May 1997, his dresser drawers still had his clothes folded away. Anyone who did not know would still think the room was occupied. I do not know why we left his room this way. I think it was a way for us to not accept what happened.

We began to pack every piece of his room away while we told stories of better times when Eric was here. My cousin Tammy was holding Eric's diploma from his high school graduation in her hand, and she was ready to put it in a box when it flew out of her hands. I was watching her when this happened and there was nothing physical around that would have done that. Suddenly the atmosphere in the room changed, and we could feel Eric's presence in the room with us. We realized that the tassel was on the dresser so possibly he wanted those items boxed together.

Eric's entire room was packed up and empty and the only thing left was his bed that was still made. For forty-three years his bed was made with his sheets and comforter tucked neatly around his pillows just the way he made it. Travis quickly ripped all the blankets off the bed and shoved them into the dumpster. This was the hardest experience in this whole house. I felt like a huge band aid was just ripped off my heart and it was at that very moment that I could feel everything, every emotion. And just like that it was done, the house was empty.

The house now was empty

This is the point where my investigation began. The house was completely empty, and it was the night before the papers to sell the house were to be done. Once it began to get dark out, I had everyone leave for a few hours. I needed to do this investigation on my own for one last time. I also needed this time to say my final farewells to the house and to the spirits that I grew up knowing so very well. For my investigation I used a voice recorder, a ghost box, and a Mel meter with REM. I wanted to keep the equipment very minimal for this investigation because this was a more personal investigation.

I began by walking room by room while I told stories that I remembered in the house. It may sound like I was talking to myself, but I knew that there were several spirits in the house that were listening to me. While I was sitting on the floor in what used to be the playroom for my brother and I, I could hear very loud footsteps from the dining room coming toward me. I did not feel much else or witness much in the downstairs of the house during my investigation other than the footsteps that I had heard.

I then began to go upstairs, and with each step, memories just flooded my mind of all the paranormal experiences that I had in that house growing up. I was ready to turn on the ghost box when I heard what sounded like a loud swoosh go by my face, and I could feel a cool breeze rush by me. If someone was trying to get my attention, that definitely worked.

My bedroom would be where I decided to begin my investigation for the upstairs portion of the house. It was so strange to sit there with my room completely empty. It was now just a box with bare walls, an empty closet and a clean floor. It may seem crazy, but as I sat there, I still felt like the room was full. I still envisioned my room the way it was. The first thing that I asked in my room with the ghost box was "What did I used to see in here?" Immediately I received the response "Ghost!" The response was very accurate for what I used to see in my room.

As I sat in my room on the floor, I clearly heard someone coming up the stairs. I waited a moment as I listened for whoever it was to announce themselves. I then figured it was my dad and Travis coming back to the house so I stepped out of my room and into the hallway to greet them because I could still hear them coming up the stairs. To my astonishment there was nobody there. I was so certain that it was a real person that I even ran downstairs to make sure no one was there. The house was empty, not a soul except for my own.

Back up the stairs I went to continue my investigation. By this time, the house was beginning to get dark as the sun continued to set. Once I reached the landing of the upstairs hallway there was a sound that I can only describe as a person wheezing from deep in their lungs. The sound was so loud, and it came from right next to me. I played the moment back on my voice recorder and the sound was noticeably clear, along with my surprised reaction right after I had heard it.

The final room that I wanted to investigate was my brother Eric's bedroom. I brought the deed to the house up to his room with me and I sat on his floor reading the deed to the house. I felt that the best way to investigate my brother's room was to just sit there and talk to him. I talked about the house and any memory that came to mind. This was a very peaceful and enjoyable time for me. Toward the end of my investigation, I just sat in his room in complete silence for about twenty minutes. Later that week I replayed all my audio and during my time that I sat in silence there was either a lady or child's voice that said very loudly "I DO!" I do not know what they were answering "I do" to, but it was clear. Honestly, the spirits may have just been carrying on their own conversations that had nothing to do with me being there.

After investigating my brother's room, I felt a sense of closure. I did not get any answers from my brother on this investigation, but I was OK with that. I needed that time alone in the big empty house to say my final goodbyes. I began to pack up my ghost-hunting equipment that I had used. Once packed I shouted out one final farewell as I reached the front door for the final time.

December 4, 2020, was the day that we said farewell to the Preston Residence, but that is not the end of the story for this house. A new era also began on that day. Stan and Michelle Von Strohe became the new owners of the house that day. Stan and Michelle are the owners of Smoky Valley Distillery in downtown Marquette, Kansas. Conveniently my dad's house that they purchased is located directly across the alley behind the distillery.

The years began to take a toll on the house, and room by room more work needed to be done. I could not have asked for a better family to purchase my dad's house. The new owners plan on renovating the entire house to bring it back to its original glory. Once the work is complete, they plan on opening the house back up as the Haunted Preston Airbnb. So, what would have been a heartbreaking farewell ended up being a comforting happy ending and beginning.

Stan walked through each room of the house with me and had me tell him stories from my childhood with my brother Eric and me. The stories consisted of some of my best memories in the house, and of course many haunted memories. I think of the movie "Titanic" where it was under water and black and white. Rose walks to the staircase and Jake steps out and the ship comes back to life with color and beauty. I picture it to be like that when I go back to see the house redone.

Work has now begun on the house and Stan keeps me up to date with pictures and stories. I am thankful that he has invited us to stay at the house when we come back to Kansas to visit. They began to rip down all the wallpaper in the house and made a discovery on the walls going up the stairway. Underneath the wallpaper they found where my brother had signed his name Eric and age nine, and I signed my name Melissa and age six. I do not remember us signing this, but it meant the world for me to see this. I can only imagine what the future holds for the Preston house. These walls hold so many memories that I will always hold close to my heart. May the stories of this house live on.

New owners Stan and Michelle Von Strohe

CHAPTER 5

BLACKFORD COUNTY JAIL
HEARTFORD CITY, INDIANA

By Craig Nehring

Blackford County Jail

Our second stop on our investigation for day two just after the Asahel Stone Mansion was this jail. Both properties are owned by the same people and they also manage Randolph Asylum, which you can find in our book *Archives of a Ghost Hunter* Volume 2. It was about an hour's drive to this location from the mansion, and of course it was still very cold out and would get colder in the night.

We arrived a little early and parked in the parking lot across the street to wait for the host to show us around the jail. I noticed a couple of people flying a drone not far from us. They had paranormal shirts on from another team. I had totally forgotten that the haunted Monroe House is just down the block from the jail, and you could see that. I heard about that place being haunted as human bones were found in its basement. I wanted to book there but never did. I relaxed in the car since we didn't get much sleep at the mansion. The rest of the team being younger than me and having more energy jumped out of the car to take pictures of the jail and walk around town a little bit. I noticed while they were gone a car pulled up along the jail, and l walked over to see if it was our guide. In fact it was. I said to him the rest of our team should be back shortly from their walk around town. He told me while I was waiting to bring my equipment in that he would wait for them. I got everything inside and sat in the jail's kitchen in the back of the jail that was nicely stocked with every food you could imagine. It was as if they stocked up in case of a lockdown because of COVID-19 or some other disaster, but it looked like a good idea. If I owned a jail, I would probably stock up too and use it as a shelter from the zombie apocalypse that would soon follow. I didn't get to relax long as the rest of the team was back, and we were ready for our tour.

He started us in the kitchen and stated that this was where the officers would eat and do laundry. There was a little slit in the wall of the kitchen that had a hinge on it, and it opened and that was where the meals were slid though to the prisoners without having to go over to the cells. The kitchen led out to an area with lower cells; you had to walk down a corridor that turned a corner and then go down the row of cells. At the end of the cells was a common area with a table where maybe the inmates would sit and chat or eat. There was a pay phone in there to make calls. Each cell had a bed and toilet and not much else. We could sleep in these cell beds if we wanted to, and I think only two members stayed in them that night. We came back out of the cell area and the guide explained to us the big wheel on the outside of the cell. The wheel would turn and lock or unlock the prisoners in their cells without having a key to go to each cell, which also made it safer and involved less interaction with the inmates. The room just outside this area had all the radios in there for calls coming in and out of the jail like emergency calls or to report crimes. A staircase sat just off that room and went to the next level. There was a heated back bedroom, which was for the main family that ran the jail and had TV and some furniture to relax. This is where some of the people who take care of the place now stay.

The next level up had a few bedrooms and an attic. The bedrooms were cozy, and we could sleep in them for the night. I picked one of the rooms there to sleep in comfort rather than a hard jail cell bed. The attic was cold and not insulated, and you could hear kids down on the street. Now tonight was Halloween and we figured we would have to determine which were inside and outside noises. There were a couple of small rooms upstairs as well used for interrogation. There was one more set of stairs that was rather steep going up to another level, and we headed up the stairs to find the top of the jail or another attic area. There was a rope noose from where they would hang people and a trap door that would open to drop them to break their neck in the hanging. The tour guide said that there was some activity up there with the noose.

We had one more stop and that was the basement, which was said to be the most haunted since they would put prisoners down there in solitary confinement. The basement was off the kitchen and through the back of the pantry area and down a flight of stairs. The first room had a small room that was called the evidence room and there was still evidence down there like baseball bats and the crimes were listed on the bat for what it was used for.

The noose in the top part of jail used for hangings

We then headed back further into the basement to some other rooms, and one of the rooms had a dirt floor with some equipment in it and a few shovels like someone was looking for something. The legend states that there are trolls that have been seen in that room, sort of like elves if you believe in that type of stuff. The next room had very narrow corridors that the average person would find very claustrophobic. They would take the prisoners and put them back here in a cell that was down a corridor and around the corner. I was very creeped out by these narrow passageways all made from concrete. There was no way two people could go in two different directions without heading back to the junction to wait for the other person to get by. The corridors went for a ways and then turned a corner and down another corridor to a dead end. I was thinking someone could meet their end in one of these narrow passageways. It was going to be an interesting investigation down here tonight.

That was the last stop, so we headed upstairs, and the host turned us loose. We decided to order some pizza and some of the team went to pick it up in town since no one was delivering yet. It was a good time to get the equipment ready and get ready for the investigation and go over some of the history of the jail to see if we were looking for anyone to call out to while we investigate. On the investigation that night would be Kara, Brittnie, Jennifer, Lisa, Danyelle, Drew, Jason, and myself.

The History of Blackford County Jail

The old Blackford County Jail was established in 1879. The prison was active until the end of 1995.

Hartford City, Indiana, began in the late 1830s as a few log cabins clustered near a creek. The community became the county seat of Blackford County. This small farming community experienced a fifteen-year "boom" beginning in the late 1880s caused by the discovery of natural gas.

Many stories linger to this day about Dillinger staying at the prison.

I could not find much more on the history of the jail.

The Investigation of the Jail

We started in the cell area by sitting in the cell beds to see if something would join us. I once had this happen at Mansfield Prison so we were hoping it might happen here too. We were greeted by some heavy footsteps coming down the jail cells' hall and that was followed by a whispered sigh. It got quiet after that, and we decided to send the women upstairs and we would head down to the tunnels in the basement to see what we could hear. We stopped by the evidence room and heard a scream but that had come from outside on the street somewhere. Nothing more was heard in the area of that room.

We headed back to the corridors that made me very uneasy. Two of us sat outside the corridor, but I sat inside it which might have been a mistake. It was pitch black and the only way for anything to get in or out would be through me. We started asking questions and thought we heard a noise down one of the passageways but not sure where. I sat there in the entrance still and heard a loud breath of air behind me followed by the brushing against the cement walls. I jumped up and said "Nope," I was not sitting there any longer. The rest of the team down there next to me heard it as well but couldn't make out what it said or was. I had the bright idea that we split up in the passageway and of course everyone volunteered me to go down to the very end, the furthest away from everyone. I made my way down to the end and stood there with a flashlight off but ready to turn on in a moment's notice. Drew was in the middle where it opened and likely felt the safest there. Jason was at the very end and had the easiest of paths to escape harm. We started by asking questions with of course no replies, and it was oddly quiet for what some say is a highly active area. I was still feeling very uneasy stuck at the end of the passage. It felt like something tugged my shirt and maybe had a little more confirmation since Drew said something grabbed him and he needed to get out of there. I was not going to stay there by myself, so we all headed out of the passageways. I was the last one out and had the feeling something was going to grab me and pull me back in and hide me forever. It was OK and we were fine. We stayed down there a bit longer, but everything seemed to be quiet. We headed upstairs to see how the women were doing and they said other than footsteps everything was quiet. We took a break to enjoy some more pizza and hang in the kitchen where there was some heat coming from a vent.

We were ready to get back to investigating. We all headed upstairs this time and a couple of us were in the attic and some were in some of the bedrooms. I heard what sounded like a knock on the wood beams in the attic but other than some kids down on the street nothing more was heard. The bedrooms the rest were sitting in were also noticeably quiet. We headed up the last flight by the noose in the hanging area, and even though we asked some questions to get answers there were none. I tried the ghost box but even that turned out nothing that wanted to communicate with us. Maybe it was just an off night. I was cold and headed down to the kitchen to warm up, and the rest of the team wanted to give it one last shot. It was like an hour they were gone to investigate, and they came back and met me in the kitchen. Nothing happened for them at all, no noises, just quiet. I went over the audio on my recorder and other than a few noises like the breath of air and cement making noise when someone was moving in the passageway, no other voices were caught on audio, for us that is rare. We decided to call it a night and head off to bed as we needed to drive home in the morning. I woke after a good night sleep and found everyone to be gone. I was alone. Hello, man down. I guess the motto "no one left behind" went out the window. I am glad the ghosts stayed quiet now that I was alone with no one to hear me scream.

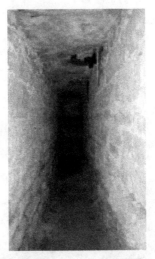

Long passageway in the basement

CHAPTER 6

Ruth Ann Miller Shrine Calumet, Michigan

By Melissa Clevenger

Ruth Ann Miller Shrine

The story of Ruth Ann Miller is an incredibly sad and tragic one. It is important to point out that we treat those who have passed with upmost respect and curtesy when we are investigating. I would hope that anyone who is reading this book would never vandalize a site or trespass. It is unfortunate that these things do happen. We are covering this investigation to honor little Ruth Ann Miller.

The Copper Country is one of my favorite places to go. My mother and her family lived in Copper City, Michigan, when she was younger, and my grandma still owns the house there. With every trip that I travel there, I always make sure to pay my respects to Ruth Ann Miller at her peaceful little shrine.

The History of the Ruth Ann Miller Shrine

Just north of Calumet, Michigan, is a copper mine that was called the Tamarack Mine. The Tamarack Mine was an underground copper mine. In 1882, the first shaft was mined, and in all it consisted of five shafts that were mined for copper through the years. Each shaft was driven vertical, during the development stage. The deepest of the five shafts ended at 5,309 feet from the surface.

Tamarack Number Four was approximately 12 feet by 18 feet wide with a depth of 4,400 feet deep. Mining operations had ceased at Tamarack Number Four in 1931. In 1936, they placed a plug of concrete 1,100 feet into the mine shaft, and a concrete slab was placed over the entrance.

On July 16, 1966, Ruth Ann Miller was picking berries with her ten-year-old brother and another friend. Throughout the year erosion began to create a hole by the cap that sealed the mine shaft. Seven-year-old Ruth Ann got too close to the hole and fell in. A three-day rescue effort quickly began.

I remember my grandmother always telling the story of little Ruth Ann Miller. She went to the site every day during the rescue efforts with the Salvation Army. They stayed by the workers and served them sandwiches and drinks throughout the day. It was an extremely dangerous and treacherous rescue effort.

Day after day rescue workers entered the hole in hopes of reaching the little girl. As the rescue workers tried to remove the concrete cap, it began to break apart and fell into the hole making rescue efforts even harder. It was soon realized that the concrete slab had become lodged at 500 feet and there was no way for the men to remove it. The hard decision was finally made that there was no way that Ruth Ann could have survived, and recovery became too dangerous. The shaft was then permanently sealed, and a high fence was installed, which made this Ruth Ann's final resting place.

This horrific incident raised awareness in the Copper Country about the dangers of unsealed mineshafts. It became a priority to securely cap all the abandoned mine shafts throughout the region so that this kind of a tragedy would not happen to anyone else. In 1988, Ruth Ann's mother passed away. She was laid to rest next to her daughter's final resting place.

Unfortunately, through the years the shrine has had many instances of vandalism. The original sign that told the story of what happened was shot at with a gun. The family had to replace this sign. Many years later, someone vandalized the site by jumping over the high fence and stealing one of the vases that was screwed tightly in. It is so sad to hear about these instances and so disrespectful. This site is where a little girl lost her life, and her family will never be the same.

At the shrine there is a large sign with Ruth Ann's picture that explains the tragedy of that fateful day in 1966. There is also a sign that reads: Your life's brief journey ended at this deep and lonely mine but oh, little Ruth Ann Miller it is now a cherished shrine.

The story of the Ruth Anne Miller tragedy

The Investigation of the Ruth Ann Miller Shrine

This is a memorial site that I pay my respects to every time that I visit the Calumet area. This trip included Travis, Craig, Savannah, and me. We used little equipment to conduct this investigation since it was an outdoor setting somewhat in the middle of nowhere. A voice recorder and our ghost box were the only equipment that we would be using.

We began with the ghost box by asking a few questions. Due to the desolate location, radio stations were not coming in at all on the ghost box. We then asked if Ruth Ann was there, and the reply on the ghost box was clearly "yes." What was interesting was it wasn't a little girl's voice answering us, or even a lady's voice like her mother; basically all the responses we received were in a man's voice.

We then asked who fell into the mine shaft here, and the man's voice answered "Ruth." I said out of astonishment, "Did it just say Ruth?" to which the man's voice replied with "Yes, I did." The answers we were receiving were truly clear, and they were clearly replying to our questions. I will note that other than getting solid responses to our questions on the ghost box, we did not feel any presence at this site. This site was very peaceful and beautiful.

We did not investigate for awfully long but did ask a few more questions. I then said "Ruth Ann, sweetie, how old were you when this accident happened?" This was the first and only response that we received an answer in a little girl's voice that we believe was Ruth Ann. The little girl's voice replied "eight." What is interesting here is that we know that Ruth Ann was seven when the accident happened. I then said I thought she was seven when this happened, and the little girl said on the ghost box, "I was eight."

After the little girl's response of "I was eight", I noticed the dates on the headstone inside the fenced-in area. Ruth Ann Miller was born on July 26, 1958, and she passed away on July 16, 1966. She would have been only ten days away from her eighth birthday! I found this interesting that she says that she was eight, but I suppose if I were a little kid that close to my birthday, I would say the same thing.

Ruth Ann Miller's headstone

After we received the response from what we believed to be Ruth Ann, the remainder of our questions were all answered by the man's voice. I have been trying to understand why a man would be answering every question that we asked. The only answer that I can come up with is that maybe one of the men who tried to rescue her is forever protecting her resting place. This was a comforting thought.

In the distance we could see that a storm was coming in quickly, so we decided to end the investigation and head back to our cabin. Places where tragedies happened are never easy to investigate, especially when they happen to a young innocent child. After this investigation I feel that Ruth Ann Miller is protected and watched over to this day. Her loss hopefully saved countless other lives because of the awareness that it brought to abandoned mine shafts.

Angels that keep watch over Ruth Ann Miller

CHAPTER 7

THE COTTAGE CAFÉ
PLOVER, WISCONSIN

By Craig Nehring

The Cottage Café

I have had many investigations in the Plover area of Wisconsin and happened to come across this café, which was known to be haunted. It was run by another paranormal team and a business of theirs as well as a place to investigate. We were there once for a team investigation but in 2021 we hosted a few tours here that had quite a bit of activity.

When you see this place from the outside it looks bigger than it is on the inside. Walking in the side door, you end up in the kitchen where some of the delicious meals were made when it was open for business. There is a back hallway that goes to a couple of dining rooms and in one of the dining rooms a player piano is located. The other dining room is closer to the kitchen and the small area where the milkshakes were made and the display area that might have housed some delicious pies. There is a walkway that goes to the last little dining area and is close to the owner's office. The last dining area has a bookcase and games for the customers who brought kids to give them something to do till their meals came. There is a bar right across from that dining area where drinks were served. The staircase that is around a corner leads up to the second floor, where there is a bathroom and a shower. They have two conference rooms, a large one and a smaller one, to have presentations. They have a wedding dress up there that they got from a barn where the dress wearer had committed suicide, and now this crazy haunted object resides in this café. Just outside the kitchen is a narrow staircase that leads downstairs to a couple of rooms that house some of the equipment used to run a restaurant along with saltshakers and vases and much more. We had two events here and helping with these events were John, Jeremy, Kara, Drew, and Rebecca.

The History of the Cottage Café

The building was built in the 1850s, and had twelve previous owners, and has been everything from a private residence to a hotel to restaurants. Long ago, the Sowiak family resided in the building. Although they never publicly talked about the house being haunted, one of the children of the family remembers feared one of the upstairs bedrooms. Before the Sowiak family, the Pierce family lived there. James Pierce, the father, was a deacon of the local church and outwardly talked about the evils of alcohol. This became apparent when the building was home to the Sherman Restaurant, where glasses would fly off the bar. Renovations to the building allowed for the ghostly residents to stir up trouble, including slamming doors, shattered windows, flying plates, and more happening daily in the restaurant.

Today, the owners of the building, now the Cottage Café, are sisters who are paranormal investigators and say that the ghosts are friendly and always welcomed in the building. Although the café is no longer in- use for daily dining, spooky events are held there often, especially near Halloween!

The Investigations

We had two separate events here with guests, and some of the things that happened were interesting. One of our helpers Rebecca is getting married soon. We were sitting upstairs when she decided to walk up to the wedding dress and say that it was a pretty dress and she wanted to wear it. She said she felt weird after saying that and the meters we had below the dress started going off to alert us that there was a ghost close to the dress and likely close to Rebecca. Whatever was over there did not want her close to it, and when she tried to touch it something touched her, so she backed away. Some of the other investigators were downstairs, and they were getting touched by something in the basement and around the location of their ankles. It is noted that there is a ghost cat or two that reside in the café and have been caught on camera by the team that runs the place. We had a couple of knocks and bangs upstairs and a few spots that got cold that we couldn't explain. We headed back downstairs when things got quiet and investigated the dining areas to see if we could capture anything there at all. There was a noise that sounded like a glass was moved but we couldn't find anything out of place.

We switched investigation areas and headed to the basement to see what we could capture down there. I had a static bear, but nothing seemed to want to touch him tonight. A few years back in the basement I saw red eyes on my video camera, yet nothing was there to the naked eye. Was this the cat that likes to hang out here or something more than just the cat? We dropped back into one of the corridors where there was lots of stuff stored. There were two chairs in there, and I sat on one while Rebecca sat on the other. It was quiet so I turned on the ghost box and said "Hello" and the minute I said it, a female voice replied with a "Hello," which was cool. There seemed to be a whisper that came from somewhere within the area we were at but couldn't make out what it said and never picked it up on audio. It was a cold night outside and below zero so we liked to stay on the upper floors, and it was just about time to offer the guests free roam so they could investigate on their own and see what they could capture. Jeremy and I decided to take one of the big conference rooms upstairs, where there was a heater, to stay in for a few hours till morning and then drive home. We waited a little while before turning in since guests were still there and walking around. A few of them were having some activity now that we left them on their own. A group of women were communicating with the ghost that belonged to the wedding dress, and the ghost was answering their questions. It was getting late and most of the guests left and the remaining ones were talking with the owner and using some of her ghost hunting devices down by the bar and told us to go get some sleep. I had a cot on one side of the room and Jeremy was on the other side. I thought as I was dozing off to sleep that something kicked my cot, but it was something I couldn't see. I was way too tired at that time to care but noted it to Jeremy who was still awake enough to hear me say it.

We both made it home the next day, and I was beat and needed some sleep that night. I went to bed early but really didn't feel like myself and had almost the same feeling I had when I had an attachment many years ago. I found this odd since the café seemed to have nice ghosts there. Just when I was about to fall asleep, I heard a women's voice say something in my bedroom but couldn't make out what she had said. I still felt weird when I woke up and decided to sage myself and call someone to do a clearing on me. I called Jeremy to tell him as well, and he said he had something weird happen too. He said that it sounded like a leaf had fallen on the floor in his room and he also felt something brush against his mustache to the point where he had to feel it because his first instinct was that a mouse had run across his face. He had to check to see if it was there, but nothing was there and nothing more happened after that. My computer had also turned itself on in the middle of the night, and it has never done that. It was on sleep mode, which means something would have had to touch it to get it to turn on. I had my clearing, and since that night nothing more had happened.

Second event had one new investigator we hadn't seen in a while. John was over from Gresham to hang out and investigate with us. He had a thermal camera and was showing all the guests who just showed up how it worked. I had just gotten my thermal camera and was using it as well. I had ordered pizza for our guests and was waiting for that to arrive so everyone could eat while it was still warm. Door Dash got there with the pizza, only they had most of my order wrong. I was missing three pizzas and two of the pizzas that came were thin crust, which I hadn't ordered at all. One of the pizzas looked like the delivery guy had sat on it as it was all stuck to the top of the box. I called and complained so they had to send two more pizzas. We didn't want to wait forever so I sent guests up with John and the rest with Jeremy while I waited for the pizza. The pizza came about thirty minutes later, and I called to everyone to come eat. They said it was pretty quiet other than Kara having something rub up against her leg; she thought it might have been the cat.

We sat there eating pizza and the owner came out to play the player piano for us. While doing it she was getting a workout. I remember player pianos, but I saw them play on their own. The owner had to pump this one to get it to work since she didn't have the one that played on its own. We all heard a loud thump come from upstairs, yet no one was there. Maybe they were happy that someone was playing the piano and maybe they missed the music, or they wanted to dance. We were waiting for everyone to finish their pizza so we could head back upstairs and investigate in the conference room.

One of the dining areas by the bar

Round two takes us upstairs where some of the guests started to communicate with what we believe was the cat by using cat toys and calling the cat. The K2s were going off closer to the floor by the girls' legs. We tried to debunk it as electricity in the floor, but we could not. Every time they used the cat toy or called the cat, it seemed to come. I was using my thermal but not catching anything over by them, which didn't mean that it is not there but just that my thermal was not picking it up. This went on for like an hour, which also included some knocking noise on the wall. The hallway with the wedding dress remained quiet; there was no one there that was getting married soon, and maybe that was why it was not active this weekend. We decided to take a break and head downstairs and get more pizza.

I handed out a few things to guests including a static bear to the girls who were talking to the cat upstairs. We went downstairs but it was incredibly quiet and nothing this time was happening although the other group said that they were having activity down here. We stayed down a while to let the group upstairs have some time. We then traded spots, and I had people split up upstairs into some of the smaller rooms. The girl was now holding my bear hostage in hopes that the cat would want to free it. The cat did come to play again with that group, and they were throwing the cat toy, which would make noises as if something was indeed playing with it. That whole thing of playing with the cat went on for about an hour. They came out of the room. Just as they came out there was a light that looked like an old lantern on the wall, and it banged against the wall, yet no one had touched it at all. We again tried to recreate it but the only way it would have moved was if someone had touched it, and no one had. It again was getting late, and we needed to allow them free roam again. We stuck around for about an hour more but by then most guests had left. There were a few that were staying till like 4:00 am. I wanted to get to bed so the owner said she can watch them. We made it home safely and nothing was heard from that weekend at my house. It sounds like they are going to move the house to a different section of the town, and I wonder if activity will pick up because they are changing its location. I guess we will have to find out some time.

CHAPTER 8

Calumet Theatre
Calumet, Michigan

By Melissa Clevenger

Calumet Theatre

I spent a fair amount of my childhood in the Upper Peninsula of Michigan and grew to love the area. During my younger years, my time there was spent going on adventures with my brother, Eric. As I grew older, I fell in love with the natural beauty of the copper country. It is no surprise that I began to dig into the paranormal history of the Upper Peninsula.

I had read stories about the Italian Hall Disaster, but I knew that the actual building was no longer standing. Through my research I learned about the history of hauntings that have occurred at the Calumet Theatre. With the theatre's connection to the Italian Hall Disaster by serving as a makeshift morgue, it became a location that I was intrigued to investigate.

The History of the Calumet Theatre

The Calumet Theatre was built in 1900 and is also known as the Calumet Opera House. On March 20, 1900, the theatre opened, attracting some of the best actors and actresses. Calumet was a rich mining community so the theatre stayed busy, but through the years the economy began to decline causing the theatre to lose popularity. In 1971, the Calumet Theatre gained a spot on the National Register of Historic Places and was made a Michigan State Historic Site.

Many visit the Calumet Theatre in hopes of catching a glimpse of the ghost of Madame Helena Modjeska. It has been told that in 1958, an actress named Adysse Lane had forgotten her lines during a performance. Adysse said that when she forgot her lines the ghost of Madame Helena Modjeska appeared to her and helped her with her lines. Numerous other unexplained occurrences have happened since then. The banquet hall in the theatre became a makeshift morgue in 1913 for the lost lives of the Italian Hall Disaster.

In Northwest Michigan one of the biggest copper mining companies in the Keweenaw Peninsula was the Calumet and Hecla Mining Company. In 1913, one of the areas, longest strikes occurred that included the Calumet and Hecla Mining Company. The strike would continue from July 23, 1913, and would not end until April 1914.

Looking down the sidewalk to the theatre

On Christmas Eve, December 24, 1913, the Ladies Auxiliary of the Western Federation of Miners held a party for the miners on strike and their families along with other people in the community. This Christmas party was held at the Italian Benevolent Society Building, which is better known as the Italian Hall, with an attendance of well over 600 people. During the hard times of the strike the Christmas party was meant to bring some joy to the families along with gifts for the many children in attendance.

While many of the children were either watching a play or standing in line to receive their Christmas gift, and hundreds of people were upstairs, an unknown man yelled "fire" at the top of his lungs. Panic instantly ensued throughout the crowd of hundreds as the push for the doors began. Chaos erupted as people began to fall from the stairs and bodies began to be trampled over. The doorway at the bottom of the stairs began to pile up with bodies as they were slammed against the closed doors making the doors impossible to open. A bottleneck of bodies quickly built up at the base of the stairs as more people began to be trampled on and suffocated. The entire hallway was quickly blocked by bodies.

After the horrific incident crews began to clear out bodies from the hall piling them in the back of the building outside. In total seventy-three people lost their lives, and out of that fifty-nine of them had been children. Out of the fifty-nine children that passed away that day, the youngest victim was only two years old. Buildings close by began to be used as makeshift morgues for all the casualties. What began as a joyous holiday soon became a nightmare as the families that were left to grieve had to begin planning the funerals of their loved ones.

Rumors began to surface that the exit doors at the bottom of the stairs in the hall were designed to open inward. If that rumor were true it would explain why the trapped people couldn't get out because it caused them to be pressed against the doors as people were crushed further preventing the doors to be opened. The search began for the man who falsely yelled "fire" during the celebration. It was thought that the man was from the anti-union ally of mine management, and he was trying to disrupt the party. This mysterious man who caused so much havoc and ended so many innocent lives was never found; his identity remains a mystery to this day.

Coffins began to be express shipped to Calumet for the seventy-three deceased victims. The massive funeral procession took place on December 28, 1913. The funeral drew in over 20,000 spectators, and 500 miners from other Upper Peninsula towns came to join in the procession. A chorus of hymns were sung by many of the miners on strike and a brass band played throughout the procession.

In October 1984, the Italian Hall was demolished with only the sandstone and brick archway to remain. The memorial has a plaque that tells the story of the Italian Hall Disaster, and later a ten-foot-tall memorial was installed to list the name and age of each of the victims from that fateful day.

The investigation of the Calumet Theatre

The Calumet Theatre is a place that my mother used to go to when she was younger, and I had always wanted to go to it. As we pulled up and began to get our suitcases of equipment from the back of my vehicle, I couldn't help but look up at the magnificent old building. So much history, so many people have gone through those doors throughout the years. Just before we made it to the side door of the building, the owner met us with a friendly "hello" in his bold Texan voice. We entered the theatre, and he led us right on the stage to begin our tour. This place was stunning, I couldn't help but gaze off into the empty seats in front of me as the owner began to tell us about the history.

We were told the stories of Madame Helena Modjeska, who is said to haunt the place, along with the story of the Italian Hall Disaster and how the banquet hall was used as a makeshift morgue for all the victims. We were also told countless stories of the famous people who have performed in the building throughout the years. The tour was very fascinating, and the building was more than I expected. Now I was ready for what we really came here for, to investigate.

This investigation would include Craig, Travis, Savannah, Savannah's daughter, and myself. It was now time for "lights out" and for our investigation of the Calumet Theatre to begin. We decided to begin in the theatre, so we spread out and each took a seat in the audience. We sat the REM pod on the stage along with another voice recorder, and we began to ask a variety of questions.

The inside of the Calumet Theatre

A few of us in the group began to have ringing in our ears and we all described our heads as feeling heavy. I do not know what caused this feeling, but at times for me it got so intense that it was almost intolerable. After about thirty minutes of pure silence, other than our questions, we decided that the girls in the group would head up on the stage to continue our investigation while the boys stayed in the audience.

At one point, Craig said "Marco," hoping for the response of "Polo." I began laughing as I said, "The ghost is probably like, oh my gosh it's the Marco Polo Guy, he really does exist." Craig is known for always saying "Marco Polo" at every-haunted location that we investigate at, so I am beginning to wonder if he is famously known by ghosts everywhere as the Marco Polo Guy.

On stage we continued to ask more questions, but there was still silence. Craig then said if anyone is on stage with us then please set off the REM pod that is by the girls. Just then the REM pod went off with its bright lights and noise right on cue. After what seemed like an hour of silence, I then decided we should be a little silly. We have found through our years of investigating that sometimes we get the best evidence when we are simply being ourselves.

I decided that it might be best to pretend like we were putting on a show for the audience. We began by finding some older music from the 1940s, and I danced silly on stage along with Savannah and her daughter. We were laughing so hard, and if there were any ghosts in the audience, I can only imagine what they thought of us.

After we were done with our funny song and dance, we decided to take a bunch of group pictures throughout the theatre area. These pictures consisted of a variety of funny ones along with some serious professional pictures. We felt like our investigation of the theatre area was complete so we then all headed to the lower-level dressing room that many famous artists have used throughout the years.

The dressing room had a completely different feel to it, almost a creepy feel. The seats in the dressing room made a square where everyone would face each other if they sat down. As we each took our seats, I carefully sat my voice recorder on the table beside me. All around us were full-sized mirrors, which in the darkness added to the creepy appeal of the room.

Craig turned on the ghost box and we began to ask questions. We like to always begin our ghost box sessions by saying "hello." Instantly a man's voice said "hello" back to us. In the beginning all the responses we were receiving were very normal, and then everything changed. The responses on the ghost box began to tell us a story of a murder that happened in the basement of the building. We were told about a man who was shot and was still buried in the basement today.

Everything that we asked about this supposed murder received a response that built to the story. The atmosphere of the dressing room by this time had begun to feel a little terrifying. At one point a response on the ghost box clearly said, "Look out!" There are no reports of such a death, let alone someone being buried in the basement. We do believe that sometimes ghosts will say things just to play with you or to make you scared. We do not know if that is the case here; it seemed so bizarre with some of the things that were coming out of the ghost box.

Prior to our investigation our tour guide led us into the basement area for a few minutes. The basement area consisted of extremely low ceilings and spider webs, was pitch dark and had dirt floors. Everything that you would need for the perfect horror story. Of course, Travis and Craig were dying to investigate the basement area! The girls on the other hand would opt out of this part of the investigation.

We asked with the ghost box on if Travis should go investigate the basement now, and we received the response of "yes, Travis." Since Craig was going to investigate with him, we then asked if Craig should go with Travis to the basement. The response we received for that was "no." It then said, "Craig... he is one of us." Of course, this terrified Craig because we did not know what was meant by this. What would you do if you were given a warning by a ghost to not go into the basement? Well, if you are Travis and Craig, you grab your equipment and head straight to the basement.

As the boys went to the basement, I decided that the girls should investigate in the balcony of the theatre. The balcony is where several people have reported seeing the ghost of a lady. By now it was completely dark outside and even our flashlights didn't completely pierce through the darkness inside. We spent some time in silence hoping to hear something. Unfortunately, it was just that, silent.

As Travis and Craig ventured farther into the dark basement with the dirt floor, Craig began to feel uneasy with his surroundings. Suddenly Craig winced out in pain as something scratched his upper back causing him to bleed. Upon investigation of the area, there was nothing around Craig that could have caused this deep of a scratch. Was this the ghost that warned Craig to not enter the basement during the ghost box session in the dressing room? Craig decided that he didn't want to test and see what the ghost were warning him about, so they decided to head back to the main floor of the theatre.

We all then decided to go together to the banquet hall area to conduct a thorough investigation of the hall. This was the area that was made into a makeshift morgue for many of the victims of the Italian Hall Disaster. With the number of children who lost their lives that day, we wondered if we would communicate with any of them. We do not believe that any soul would stay in a location, but we do believe that ghost can travel to wherever they want, and if they knew we had the means to communicate with them they may want to.

The banquet hall was filled with round tables surrounded by chairs to sit in. A room that I am sure has hosted many celebrations through the years after its days of being a morgue. We began to each take a seat spread out through the room. We placed different equipment and a few toys throughout the room in hopes of triggering a reaction. While we investigated, we took a different approach and talked to the ghost as if they were right there with us. While we sat and talked, we did not receive any sort of response or anything that could be considered paranormal.

To end our investigation time in the banquet hall, we slowly cited the name and age of each of the seventy-three victims from the Italian Hall Disaster. Once we got through each name, we decided to have a moment of silence to honor them. After our moment of silence, each of us got up and quietly began our exit from the banquet hall.

We were now nearing 2:30 a.m. after spending several hours investigating the theater. I think we all felt a little disappointed that more didn't happen during our investigation. Our final stop before we headed back to our cabin for the night would be the spot where the Italian Hall once stood so many years ago, before it was demolished.

As we walked toward the arch, which is the only remaining part of what was the Italian Hall, the warm breeze felt like it was almost moving us toward the memorial. One step at a time, we came closer to the ten-foot-tall marker that listed each victim's name and age. In one hand I held my voice recorder and my other hand I would place directly on the arch. Craig held the ghost box, which we used for our investigation.

We said "hi" and immediately got the response of "hi." I don't know why, but we did feel a little uneasy at the arch. A car drove by very slowly and "be scared" came across the ghost box. A voice on the ghost box then said to fear the vehicle. When I asked what vehicle, a voice said, "Blue truck." Only about one minute after the ghost box said, "Blue truck," a blue truck came around the corner and drove by us! It could have possibly been a coincidence, but we decided to not stay much longer just in case. The ghost box also said that this was a "brick portal."

There was so much energy at the site where the building once stood. The site of such a sad tragedy. We ended our investigation with a prayer for all the souls who lost their lives on that very tragic day.

Not long after returning to Wisconsin from our investigation at the Calumet Theatre, I began to go over my hours of audio that I had recorded. I really was not expecting much to come from my audio because overall we felt that the building was not overly active. Boy, was I surprised with everything that I heard.

Many of the EVPs that I captured were in the actual theatre area. There was a point when Craig was talking and between his sentences was a lady's voice whispering. Unfortunately, I was not able to determine what the whispers were saying. There was also a very strange noise that we had all heard with our ears. After listening to this noise several times, I could not figure out what the noise was. Even if a noise is strange, that does not necessarily make it paranormal. There were also a few creepy sounding whispers while we were sitting in silence in the theatre.

At one point Travis mentioned the lights that shine down on the stage, and at that point a man's voice whispered, "I do some of the lights." We also picked up a little girl's voice that says "mommy" as well as a voice that says, "girl is dead." When I was on the stage, I asked how many ghosts were in the audience. I could not believe when I went over my audio that there was an answer to my question. A man's voice whispered, "all of them," in response to my question.

I was shocked at how much evidence I received from my audio. It almost makes you wonder at any given time in the day how many ghosts are trying to communicate with us. As for the Calumet Theatre, we all had a great night investigating.

Craig, Savannah, Melissa, Travis

CHAPTER 9

FIRST WARD SCHOOL'S FINAL FAREWELL
WISCONSIN RAPIDS, WISCONSIN

By Craig Nehring

First Ward School

The First Ward school is one of the team's favorite places to go, until 2020 when everything changed because of the coronavirus. The owner of the school, Justin, has decided to call it quits and leave the good old United States behind and sell the school to someone else.

I hope whoever buys it will let us come and stay here like we always used to but that seems to never happen. It will likely become apartments because that is what every haunted location seems to become nowadays. We have been investigating this school since 2012 and had some amazing times here and even filmed U.S. Cellular commercials here in 2016. I have not found any other location that I can call home in Wisconsin. I will call this the final farewell, or it could even be the absolute best of First Ward as the stories that follow will be the most amazing ones and the best times that we had in the school. We had guests here throughout the years and many team members, some of whom are no longer with us as they moved onto different careers and some of them got so scared at this school, they left the team altogether. I heard Justin talk about the history of the school so many times that I could give the complete history without even looking at my notes.

The History of First Ward School

In the late 1800s due to overcrowding in Wisconsin Rapids public schools, the Board of Education met and agreed to build a new school in the first ward district.

The total cost of the school was $10,154. The most interesting thing about the construction of the school is that the brick they used for the building was made on site rather than being shipped to the location. They also painted the doors, gables, and classrooms in watercolor.

The school was finished in 1896 containing four large classrooms, heated by a huge coal furnace, and had all the latest technology like electricity, adjustable seats, and the best blackboards available at the time, and Venetian blinds. The First Ward School is the oldest surviving school building in Wisconsin Rapids today.

The school housed kindergarten to sixth grade and even hosted a high school grammar class. Physical education was taught in the classrooms by the teachers. The janitor did, however, teach the boys basketball in the coal room. In 1902 the pupils and teachers were told to pick a new name for the First Ward School. It was decided to name the school Irving after the author Washington Irving aka Diedrich Knickerbocker, who was extremely popular at the time.

In 1910 the bell tower was struck by lightning and burned off the building. The bell tower was never replaced, and a few years later the school was closed due to the high cost of keeping it running. The city had an $8,000 school tax but only collected half of that amount forcing the closure of the school.

In 1921 due to the increase in students in the Wisconsin Rapids area, the school was reopened but only with kindergarten to third grades. This was done by the local nuns who undertook teaching at the school themselves while living in the attic of the building. (This is why the attic doors lock from the inside.) This helped keep the cost down of running the school so the town could have the much-needed increase in classrooms. This is also where the stories of the school being haunted originated from. While living in the school the nuns noticed strange things happening in different areas of the school at different times of day. This led the nuns to come up with a plan as to when and where they would not go in the school during these times of activity. You could almost say the nuns were the first to investigate the activity in this building by keeping a log when and where activity took place. Owners are currently in the process of locating this log and finding someone who would remember this information.

In 1921, the roof of the school caught fire from one the embers from the coal furnace going out of the chimney and landing on the roof. The janitor noticed the fire while walking home to eat lunch. All the children got out in time and no one was hurt. The fire was caught early enough that the damage was repairable.

Before World War II the building was also used for a small school for the deaf run by Agnes Mader and hosted the city's first special education classes taught by Allie Marie Coon. The other teachers stayed the same over the years. Muriel Holiday, Joyce Pettis, Elaine Domask, and Ina Iverson Peterson.

In 1954 the interior of the school was remodeled. A kitchen and cafeteria were added, the bathrooms were taken out of the basement and moved upstairs, and the coal furnace was converted to gas. The cafeteria also doubled as the school's gym. After lunch they would breakdown the tables allowing the space needed for physical education.

The last year the school ran as a grade school was 1977. For two years after the building was used for exceptional education offices and classes. The building has remained vacant since 1979.

Justin bought the school in 2010 and at the time the school was being used for storage of garbage as the person that owned it at the time would flip houses and bring back all the garbage and pile it up in the school in rooms. When Justin was done cleaning the school, he had removed two tons of trash and had to repaint many of the classrooms that had graffiti on the walls by kids who would break into the school.

While in the process of doing all this, he started to notice things were not right in the school. He heard disembodied voices and saw a little girl standing over the sink in the bathroom. He also heard footsteps and heard things move in the school. His mom came for a visit and was inside the school in the basement when she was held against the wall by an unseen force and she felt like she couldn't move for a few minutes. She got out of there as fast as she could and would no longer go into the basement area or go into the school by herself.

Over the years Justin had tons of teams doing investigations including ours; and he loved the ghosts that resided there and if one of the ghosts asked for something, he would buy it for them. The little girl that asked for a blue bicycle got a blue bicycle, and he would decorate a tree for the kids and many more holidays decorations throughout the year. He always said the ghosts were once people too and he was right. He also said if you promise the ghost something always makes sure you follow through with your promise because so many teams make this mistake when they say stuff like I will give you a cookie if you move that ball for us and the ball moves but they never receive their cookie. I now make good on my promises for anything I ask in return for the ghosts to do.

He once had a skeptic in the school on the first-floor classroom, and he didn't really believe the school was haunted, but he also believed in the same thing that Justin believed in with making good on promises. He was in the classroom and he asked the children if they were in the classroom to walk over to the chalkboard and get in a long line and he would take them outside for recess. He is amazed by what he hears: footsteps come from within the room and walk over to the chalkboard. He then asks the children if they want to go outside to knock on the chalkboard that they are ready to go and he hears all these tiny knocks come from the chalkboard. He then proceeds to make good on his promise and leads the kids outside and plays with them and brings them back inside when he is done.

The classroom where the kids like to play

Investigations through the Years

One of our first investigations through the years was early on in 2012 and featured Sheila, Jason, Rick, and Julia, and like always when arriving at our destination food seems to follow. We all stopped at Taco Bell and were eating our food in one of the classrooms that had a large table in there. Some of us were done before the others, and I sent Sheila down to the basement to say hi to the ghosts that reside in the basement. She was reluctant to go on her own, but she did. We were still eating when I heard screams coming from what sounded like a few floors below. I headed downstairs to find Sheila white as a ghost. I asked her what was going on and she said she was back by the coal room when she heard what sounded like a scream of a woman.

There are a few different ghosts that reside in the school, and in the basement area we have heard a little girl who calls herself Betty; she was standing out by the curb waiting for the bus a long time ago. She was wearing a long dress and as a car passed her by the bumper of the car caught her dress and dragged her down the street to her death. The other teacher they call Miss Holiday has been spotted in the basement as well. The last person we have talked to in the basement is Mike, and he was the caretaker of the school and doesn't really like women in the area where he used to have his workshop down there. We think this was Betty screaming out to us. I went back over the audio to hear a girl's voice say, "This is Betty." Well, Sheila wanted to go back upstairs, and I headed that way as well to finish my food and then we could start the investigation with the rest of the crew. We headed up to the attic to see what we could find up there. The attic has another ghost named Oscar that had two tragic stories behind the haunting. Oscar was about eight years old and was said to have been bullied to the point that he went to the attic and hung himself, and the other story said that the bullies hung Oscar in the attic. However, this was told by many without any documentation. Through the years we had many conversations with

Oscar in the attic, and this night was no different. We were able to communicate with Oscar on the ghost box and meters were lighting up every time we talked about Oscar. We spent quite a while in the attic, and I was tired from working all day and then driving over to the school. I decided to call it a night and get some sleep in the school or so I thought I would. I was almost asleep when I heard a little girl's voice in the hallway say something, but I couldn't make it out. I then heard footsteps come into the room where I was sleeping, and someone sat down on my bed. I felt like Elliott from E.T. I opened my mouth to scream out to my team, but nothing came out. I am glad it wasn't like the movies where the blankets lift, and something comes from under the covers. I saw the indentation that it made on my bed, and I put my hand where it was at but felt nothing although it seemed cold in that spot. I jumped out of bed as I could finally move now and woke Rick, who came to check it out, but it was gone now. I still was tired and have had other encounters like this but not knowing what it was made me uncomfortable. I may not have gotten much sleep that night but there would be many more nights that are just as crazy.

The layout of the school when you walk through the front doors you are greeted by a staircase that goes up and one that goes down. One staircase leads to the kitchen and the projector room and another leads to the backside of the projector room or the other side of it. The main floor has a classroom with desks and chairs and books on every desk. Some of the books caught my attention as one was called *Gus the Friendly Ghost,* which I once had when I was a little kid. One other book was *The Handbook of Recently Deceased* and everyone knows that book from the movie *Beetlejuice*. Some desks had dolls and animals in the seats of the desks. There was a table with toys and blocks on it and a teachers' desk in the corner with a fake apple to play the part of the students giving their teacher an apple. This was one of the main classrooms with the chalkboard and in the back of the classroom was a small closet that now had a shower but back in the day was where the teacher would put students when they were bad. We heard the story of the teacher who put a student in there and forgot about him to the point that it was after school and he was still in there until someone found him to let him out. Noises can be heard coming from this closet as if someone is still locked in there.

The second floor has two classrooms back-to-back and I call one room the blue room and one the red for the colors of the rooms. The blue room; has some beds for guests to sleep in and so does the red room however, our team has always preferred the red room since the sun rises in the blue room and its so bright out in the mornings that no one can sleep in. The blue room has a dresser that the owner acquired that belonged to H.H. Holmes, who owned a hotel in Chicago that had different passageways where the bodies of many guests were found murdered; the dresser had a hidden compartment on it where he hid the murder weapons. I wonder what ghosts came with this dresser. The red room on the other side had a mummy-like bookshelf and a table and chairs; when you put your hands on the hand rests of the chairs, they would rest into finger spots. There were multiple beds for guests to sleep in here as well.

The next level went up to the attic, which was massive in size compared to any other attic I have ever been in. One side of the attic had a small out cave that had its own book library. The other side of the attic had some chairs to sit in while investigating. The whole attic was all wood with giant beams on which you could see the mason's symbols in the arch work. I was told this school was held up by the beams in the attic from the top to the bottom rather than the other way around.

The last level was going all the way downstairs that had on one side the kitchen; Justin had it decorated in red and white and it also had tons of Coca Cola antiques. There was a stove and refrigerator, but it didn't end there. The kitchen had a hot-dog maker, popcorn maker, slushie machine, and everything you could think of to make the perfect meals; and we created some awesome meals here for us and the guests over the years. One room off the kitchen had the projector in it with chairs that we used for a conference room to host our seminars here during events. The other room next to that was the boiler room and the coal room along with the laundry room.

The outside of the school also had some interesting facts to it. There used to be a cemetery on the property. They moved it when putting the street in and in fact found a few of the bodies while moving the street in; some of the bodies were never moved but the headstones were so it is possible that some of the activity is caused by this as well.

The red room where we would sleep

We had two new members on our team and the first place we took them was the school and it was a good place to train new members. They were two girls whom we had just added to the team. Now to be on the team you must have an open mind and have equipment. You also shouldn't be afraid of things that go bump in the night. Everyone gets scared from time to time, even me. We had a good night investigating and teaching them how to investigate. That night I was sound asleep, and I felt someone tap me on the shoulder. I woke up to the girls standing over me at two o'clock in the morning. They said they heard a little girl in the hallway say hello to them when they got up to go to the bathroom. I thought "Great, you guys had something happen to you that I only wish would happen to me sometimes." They said they were all leaving and not staying one more minute in that school. I said, "The girl wanted to communicate with you and you're scared from the girl saying hello. What are you going to do when something really happens." Well, they left never to return to the school again and quit the team the next day. Ghost hunting isn't for everyone and way different than watching it on TV. When you are doing real-time investigations, things are all too real for some people.

One night while investigating I was in the main classroom on the first floor; it was pitch dark and all I could see was the exit lights from the hallway. I walked to one of the couches in the room and sat down. I suddenly heard one of the toys clapping, and I knew which one it was. There was a monkey with symbols for hands that resembled the scary monkeys on Wizard of Oz and that sent every hair on my body up in the air. I knew that the monkey had no batteries in it, so why was it clapping at me? That seems to be the one thing there that I can't look at and I think the ghosts know that. Some of the other investigators were on the top floor in the attic and they were using an SLS Camera, which picks up stick figures in the dark of unseen things and maps out their body. They had captured a stick figure of a child or small person which was communicating with them; when they asked the ghost to put its hands in the air the mapping camera found the ghosts arms up in the air, which was amazing since it's hard sometimes to ask a ghost to do something and be able to back it up with evidence from a camera. I made my way out of the classroom after confirming the monkey had no batteries in it. I took a pit stop at the bathroom and should have known better always use the partner system when in the bathroom and have someone stand guard since the last thing you want to do is get caught with your pants down. I was doing my business when a toilet paper roll came flying over the top of the stall and lands on my lap. I was thinking if the ghost was trying to tell me that I stink. It would have been funnier had it been a team member but no it wasn't anyone or at least anyone that I could see. I peeked out between the cracks and nothing was there. The stall door next to me slammed shut but no one was using that stall. I then heard a sinister laugh and that got me out of the bathroom quite quick. I looked in the bathroom and there was nothing there. I caught the laugh on my voice recorder when going over it.

The monkey that likes to clap

Round two of that night took us upstairs again to the attic where they were catching stick figures on camera and decided to see if we could talk to Oscar. One of our investigators had called out to him and asked if he had been hurt up in the attic. Now there was a rope in a bucket on the other side of the room and I am not one to believe too much in orbs because most is dust but when you see a bright light with your eyes that is not on film or a camera and it hovers in the room, that will make a believer out of anyone. The light came into view on the top by the rafters where it was possible that Oscar was hung. The light moved down to the floor and dropped inside of a bucket and was gone out of sight. We walked over to the bucket and looked inside and found a rope noose that another team had made to try to reenact what could have happened to Oscar. This was another amazing thing that happened that night as we asked what happened to him and we believe this was his spirit showing us that indeed he was hung by showing us the rope in the bucket.

The attic area where we have seen Oscar

This was one of our last investigations we had at the school and maybe the last the team will have unless someone buys it that keeps allowing us to come back. We had Melissa, Travis, Savannah, and the owner of the school, Justin, there that night. We love to stay there, and I sleep well there even with the ghosts. I was on my way up one of the flights of stairs when I heard a voice say my name. I turned around but the only thing I saw was this doll standing on the staircase that has greeted us many times through the years when we would come there. I thought I was losing my mind and was wondering if it was possible someone wanted me to believe the doll talked even though it couldn't. I thought this was going to be one of those insane nights again.

The doll that I thought said something

I made my way to the red room where I would sleep for the night and everyone was sitting in there; I told them that something on the stairs had said hi to me but couldn't find out what or see anything. We relaxed for a little bit and then decided to go up to the attic and see what we can capture on the ghost box or maybe hear or see. It didn't take long for stuff to start happening when we started asking questions. There were a few loud footsteps coming up the stairs from where we had just come, and we heard them come all the way to the top. I am not sure where the ghost went to once he got to the top of the stairs, but I started to get this itchy feeling all over my chest and I have had that before when a ghost was touching me—its like I walked into an insulation barn. I didn't say anything at first and noticed that Justin was now itching too, and I asked, "Are you having the same itching feeling on your chest." He said he was, and I said I was too, and it was weird because it happened when the footsteps had stopped. The itching finally went away so we sat down by a table to turn on the device that runs white noise so the ghost can communicate, but just before we did that Melissa and Travis heard a loud scream come from close to them in the room. We replayed audio quickly and captured the scream. I then turned on the ghost box to run white noise and just for fun yelled "Marco" and the ghost yelled "Polo" back. We had a few voices come through that said Oscar and that he wanted to talk to us. I heard a few loud knocks on the wood in the back of the attic on the other side. I walked over and set up a REM pod to see if maybe Oscar wanted to touch it. It took about ten minutes and one loud knock followed by the pod going off and lighting up in all colors to tell us something was grabbing onto the antenna that was coming out of it and that was the only way it would go off. I asked whoever was touching it to please back away and the pod stopped lighting up to let me know that the ghost had backed away like I had asked. One more time I asked them to get closer to verify that it was really Oscar touching the pod and the lights all lit up again; we believe that was him communicating with us.

The school always had some highly active areas like the attic and even the kitchen downstairs, where you would hear stuff late at night. I am always up for a late-night snack and would wander down there but always had the feeling something was watching me and sometimes would hear footsteps coming up behind me while I was on the way back up the stairs. I of course increased my stride when I heard that and made it back to bed as quickly as I left. We headed downstairs to the coal room where Justin had lots of props for Halloween and most of the monsters in the coal room were very scary. There was one clown in there that seemed even scarier than the clown from that movie IT. We sat down there in some of the chairs in the room; it was a small room, so we were close together. We turned off all the lights and sat in the dark asking questions; and a few noises were heard as though something was moving around in the props. Melissa made a noise because something had touched her on top of the head and then she bumped Travis in the process, who also felt something at the exact same time. I had something touch my hand but when I looked nothing was there. We headed back up stairs to get some sleep since we had to leave in the morning, and we were tired. We enjoyed many years at this school and hope this isn't the last time we get to see it, but I am glad we had the opportunity.

Melissa, Craig, Kara, and Justin

CHAPTER 10

VILLISCA AX MURDER HOUSE VILLISCA, IOWA

By Melissa Clevenger

Villisca Ax Murder House

It was finally the day for us to leave for our trip to Villisca, Iowa, a perfect end to our action-packed week. Our week began in Calumet,

Michigan, where we investigated the Calumet Theatre, the grounds of the Italian Hall Disaster, and the Ruth Ann Miller Shrine. We spent one night at home to charge our equipment and pack and headed off for the Villisca Ax Murder House bright and early in the morning.

It's funny how quickly your excitement for a trip can fade away when you are driving the long boring roads from Wisconsin to Iowa. After a while, the cornfields begin to get repetitive, and the cows begin to not seem as thrilling. As we ventured closer to Villisca, we began to discuss our upcoming investigation and immediately the anticipation to get there returned. The scenery around us began to fill with color and vibrancy the closer we got to the tiny town. The moment I saw the giant cow statue welcoming us to Villisca, I could not help but jump out of the vehicle for a quick picture. Soon we passed the church where the family went to their final church service, and not long after we came up to the Villisca Ax Murder House.

Behind the house sits a large red barn where our tour guide, Johnny Houser, was patiently waiting for our arrival. Inside the barn were pictures, artifacts, and several newspaper articles about that fateful day. After a few moments, Johnny led us into the house through the back door. I really did not know what to expect inside the house because of the amount of fear, sadness, and tragedy that took place inside these walls. My initial thought was how tiny the house really was on the inside. The energy in the house was a little intimidating, but this was only the beginning and little did I know at the time that the energy would only get more intimidating during our two-night stay in the house.

The tour began in the kitchen, then into the living room, and finally into the bedroom that Lena and Ina had slept in that night. This completed the downstairs portion of the house. We then began to head upstairs where we came to the parents' bedroom, the attic, and finally the children's bedroom. During the tour we were told the history of the house, stories of speculations, and finally the haunted history of the house. Despite the horror of what happened in the house, the house began to have a peaceful calming feeling to it. By the time the tour was over, we were all hungry, so we decided to get something to eat before our overnight investigation. I turned on my voice recorder in the living room to record while we were gone. You never know what you will find when you go over the audio of an empty house, so I was hoping for something good. We knew we had a long night of investigating ahead of us.

The History of the Villisca Ax Murder House

In the early 1900s Villisca, Iowa, was a midwestern town of 2,500 with flourishing business and several dozen trains pulling into the station depot daily. The town name, Villisca, was said to mean "pretty place" or "pleasant view." Unfortunately, for the citizens of this close-knit community, it will be forever plagued by the horrific deaths of eight people. The Moore Family, well-known and well-liked Villisca residents, and two overnight guests were found murdered in their beds. Little known to its residents was the possibility that their town was named, not after a "pretty place" but for the Indian word "Wallisca" which means "evil spirit."

In 1994, Darwin and Martha Linn purchased the former home and returned it to its original condition at the time of the murders, June 10, 1912. There have been films and books written, but the person or persons that committed the crime was never caught and surely took their dirty secret to the grave.

On June 9 and 10, 1912, Lena and Ina Stillinger, the daughters of Joseph and Sara Stillinger, left their home for church. They planned on having dinner with their grandmother after morning service, spending the afternoon with her, and later returning to her home to spend the night after the Children's Day program concluded. The girls, however, were invited by Katherine Moore to spend the night at the Moore home instead. The Children's Day Program at the Presbyterian Church was an annual event and began at approximately 8:00 p.m. on Sunday evening, June 9. According to witnesses,

Sarah Moore coordinated the exercises. All the Moore children, as well as the Stillinger girls, participated. Josiah Moore sat in the congregation. The program ended at 9:30 p.m., and the Moore family, along with the Stillinger sisters, walked home from the church. They entered their home sometime between 9:45 and 10:00 p.m.

The following morning, at 5:00 a.m., Mary Peckham, the Moore's next-door neighbor stepped into her yard to hang laundry. At 7:00 a.m., she realized that not only had the Moores not been outside but that the house itself seemed unusually still. Between 7:00 and 8:00 a.m., Mary Peckham approached the house and knocked on the door. When she received no response, she attempted to open the door only to find it locked from the inside. After letting out the Moores' chickens, Mary placed a call to Josiah's brother, Ross Moore, setting into place one of the most mismanaged murder investigations to ever be undertaken.

Based on the testimonies of Mary Peckham and those who saw the Moores at the Children's Day exercise, it is believed that sometime between midnight and 5:00 a.m., an unknown assailant entered the home of J.B. Moore and brutally murdered all occupants of the house with an ax.

Upon arriving at the home of his brother, Ross Moore attempted to look in a bedroom window and then knocked on the door and shouted, attempting to wake someone inside the house. When that failed, he produced his keys and found one that opened the door. Although Mrs. Peckham followed him onto the porch, she did not enter the parlor. Ross went no farther than the room off the parlor.

When he opened the bedroom door, he saw two bodies on the bed and dark stains on the bedclothes. He returned immediately to the porch and told Mrs. Peckham to call the sheriff. The two bodies in the room downstairs were Lena Stillinger, age twelve and her sister Ina, age eight, houseguests of the Moore children. The remaining members of the Moore family were found in the upstairs bedrooms by City Marshall Hank Horton, who arrived shortly. Every person in the house had been brutally murdered, their skulls crushed as they slept. Josiah Moore, age forty-three, Sarah Montgomery Moore, age thirty-nine, Herman Moore, age eleven, Katherine Moore, age nine, Boyd Moore, age seven, and Paul Moore, age five, along the Stillinger Sisters.

Once the murders were discovered, the news traveled quickly in the small town. As neighbors and curious onlookers converged on the house, law enforcement officials quickly lost control of the crime scene. It is said that up to a hundred people traipsed through the house gawking at the bodies before the Villisca National Guard finally arrived around noon to cordon off the area and secure the home. These were only known facts regarding the scene of the crime:

Eight people had been bludgeoned to death, presumably with an ax left at the crime scene. It appeared all had been asleep at the time of the murders.

- Doctors estimated the time of death as somewhere shortly after midnight.
- Curtains were drawn on all the windows in the house except two, which did not have curtains. Those windows were covered with clothing belonging to the Moore's.
- All the victims' faces were covered with the bedclothes after they were killed.
- A kerosene lamp was found at the foot of the bed of Josiah and Sarah. The chimney was off, and the wick had been turned back. The chimney was found under the dresser.
- The ax was found in the room occupied by the Stillinger girls. It was bloody but an attempt had been made to wipe it off. The ax belonged to Josiah Moore.
- The ceilings in the parents' bedroom and the children's room showed gouge marks apparently made by the upswing of the ax.
- A piece of a keychain was found on the floor in the downstairs bedroom.

- A pan of bloody water was discovered on the kitchen table as well as a plate of uneaten food.
- The doors were all locked.

The bodies of Lena and Ina Stillinger were found in the downstairs bedroom off the parlor. Ina was sleeping closest to the wall with Lena on her right side. A gray coat covered her face. Lena, according to the inquest testimony of Dr. F.S. Williams, "lay as though she had kicked one foot out of her bed sideways, with one hand up under the pillow on her right side, half sideways, not clear over but just a little. Apparently, she had been struck in the head and squirmed down in the bed, perhaps one-third of the way." Lena's nightgown was slid up and she was wearing no undergarments. There was a bloodstain on the inside of her right knee and what the doctors assumed was a defensive wound on her arm.

Dr. Linquist, the coroner, reported a slab of bacon on the floor in the downstairs bedroom lying near the ax. Weighing nearly two pounds, it was wrapped in what he thought may be a dish towel. A second slab of bacon about the same size was found in the icebox.

Linquist also made note of one of Sarah's shoes which he found on Josiah's side of the bed. The shoe was found on its side; however, it had blood inside, as well as under it. It was Linquist's assumption that the shoe had been upright when Josiah was first struck, and that blood ran off the bed into the shoe. He believed the killer later returned to the bed to inflict additional blows and subsequently knocked the shoe over.

Had these murders been committed today, it is almost certain that law enforcement officials would have easily solved the crime and brought the murderer to justice. Almost 100 years later, however, the Villisca Ax Murders remain a mystery. The murderer or murderers are probably long dead, their gruesome secret buried with them. In hindsight, it's easy to blame the officials at the time for what could only be considered a gross mismanagement of what little evidence may have remained. The above information on the history of the Villisca Ax Murder House was taken from the website and was not solely my wording: http://www.villiscaiowa.com.

Some of the victims

The Investigation of the Villisca Ax Murder House

This is one investigation that I had exceedingly high hopes for. In some ways it is hard to go into an investigation that had such a horrific crime. We went into this investigation wanting to fully respect the victims, and a part of us had the hope of maybe finding out who was responsible for the murders. We knew we wouldn't solve a crime over one hundred years later, but it didn't hurt to try.

The Ax Murder House is small, so we included Craig, Travis, Kara, Savannah, and myself to conduct our two-night investigation. For five people and such a small house you would not think we would bring that much equipment. We carried five cases of equipment into the living room but used barely any of our equipment. Sometimes the best investigations are the ones where you use the least amount of equipment. For tonight, we would use voice recorders, a ghost box, REM pod, and Mel Meter with REM, and a laser grid with REM.

It was a hot day in July, so the air conditioner was constantly running in the upstairs of the house. We had to quickly make the hard decision to turn the air conditioner off so that we would not have any noise contamination. Another issue that we had before it got dark out was that people were constantly pulling up to the house to take pictures by the sign. Due to the noise contamination, we knew we would have to hold off on investigating for a little bit longer.

While we waited for it to get dark, we decided to spend some time outside taking pictures and talking to different people who came by the house. A few people were just walking right up into the house, so we had to lock the door for most of the night. Not only did this house attract people, but it also seemed to attract quite a few alley cats. The cats enjoyed hanging out on the porch of the barn, and they made every attempt to make it into the house.

Savannah, Travis, Melissa, Kara, and Craig

The time finally came where we felt it was dark and quiet outside and was now time for our investigation to begin. One by one, we slowly creeped up the stairs and into the bedrooms. The five of us divided between the parents' bedroom and the kids' bedroom. The rest of the night went slow with not much happening. Maybe the house or its occupants were just warming up to us.

The next day flew by, and before we knew it, it was already time to begin investigating again. We were all eager to see how night two would go. Once again, we decided to begin our investigation in the upstairs bedrooms. The atmosphere of the house felt a lot different tonight, and there was almost a heavy feeling in the air.

Almost instantly we began to have activity. I was sitting on one of the beds in the children's room with my legs planted on the floor in front of me. Suddenly it felt like a hand grabbed my ankle, which startled me and caused me to quickly swing my legs up onto the bed. At about the same time that my ankle was grabbed, we caught an EVP on our voice recorder saying, "follow me." Shortly after a voice whispered "Lena," which we did not hear with our ears until we went over our audio.

After a while we decided to change positions and move around. Savannah and I decided to lie in the parents' bed sideways, while Craig sat in front of the attic doors, and Kara and Travis both sat on the beds in the children's room. We asked several questions and used the ghost box for a while without getting any responses. Savannah and I began to both feel fear and anxiety. It was hard to explain, but we both felt very panicked and uneasy.

At the same time, we both said that we could smell what we could only describe as a leather and wood burning stove smell. As the smell grew stronger and stronger, so did our anxiety. It almost seemed like the smell was now over the top of us, and it was at that time that I felt a sharp pain diagonally across my chest. Savannah yelped out as she felt a sharp pain across her stomach at the exact same time as my pain. As we sat there feeling panicked, the smell of leather and wood stove overcame us. And as soon as the panic and pain started, it was gone. Pure silence filled the house, and we felt empty and alone.

The wood stove at Villisca

Every mirror in the house was covered by a blanket, which was what the killer did after the murders. We then decided to pull the blankets off the upstairs mirrors. My thought was that maybe we could connect with the family, and how they felt before the murders happened. One by one each blanket was pulled off. Savannah and I remained on the parents' bed where we had been laying. Suddenly the feeling in the air changed; the energy felt happy and light.

As we continued to lie there, I could feel the presence of a kid. I felt like it was Katherine, and she was standing right next to us by the bed. I then said, "Katherine, is that you standing by the bed?" I nearly finished my sentence when we all heard a little girl say a whole sentence! All five of us yelled out in shock at what we had just heard. We could not believe that had just happened and that it was so loud and clear. Unfortunately, we could not tell what was said at all. After our excitement at what we had just heard, we could not help but laugh. The voice seemed happy and cheerful.

Shortly after hearing the child's voice, Savannah and I both smelled something lovely right over the top of us. We could only describe the smell as rose water, and it was very prominent. We then felt like Sarah, the mother, was standing on the side of the bed. I then said, "Sarah, is that you standing by the bed?" We could not believe what happened next. We all heard what sounded like a lady laughing, and it came from right next to the bed that we were lying in. After this the room felt completely quiet and empty again. One by one we put the blankets back over each mirror in the upstairs. The experience that we had just had was so surreal, and it took us a little while to bring ourselves back to reality.

After a short break we decided to spend some time in the downstairs living room investigating. We thought it would be a good idea to leave a piece of equipment upstairs in case there was still activity up there. Craig headed up the stairs alone with the laser light with REM. He decided to set the equipment directly outside the closet door in the kids' room with the closet door opened. He then began to walk back toward the stairs where he was going to sit alone for a little bit.

Just then the REM began to go off, and Craig yelled out because he was not expecting it to go off. From downstairs, I yelled out, "If you are upstairs can you make the REM go off again please?" Right on cue the REM began to go off again, and just like before Craig yelled out in horror. I will admit, this house does have a very creepy, eerie feeling when you are all alone in it. This continued for about ten minutes with me asking the REM to go off and it going off on cue. Craig yelled and said a few not-nice words every time that it went off, and we could not help but laugh every time Craig yelled. We then decided to put Craig out of his misery and told him to come join us downstairs.

Upon going over our audio we did pick up a few EVPs while Craig was upstairs with the REM. There was a long breath of air that came from behind Craig as he was talking. Nobody was upstairs with Craig, and since he was talking this was not him. At one point a whisper said "huh." There was also a whispering voice that said a full sentence, but we were not able to determine what was said. The final thing we heard on our audio had to be replayed several times because it was so disturbing. A man's voice whispered, "I want to crack your head." This EVP was a little terrifying.

Once Craig returned downstairs, he insisted that I spend a little time alone upstairs also since I had been laughing at him yelling in fear. I obliged, because it really served me right after laughing at him, but secretly I was hoping nothing crazy would happen. Step by step I slowly made my way up the dark creepy stairs.

I decided to sit on the parents' bed, partially because it was right next to the stairway to get back downstairs. My time upstairs was quiet and uneventful. With our audio we found that after the REM went off when I was upstairs, a voice whispered, "what do you like?" I am not sure if "what do you like" was being referred to me or if it had nothing to do with any of us in the house. At one point I asked if anyone was upstairs with me and a voice responded "yes." I did not hear this with my ears, or I would have probably screamed like Craig, but it was there on my audio.

Savannah and I decided to investigate alone in the house while the other three ran to the gas station to pick up a few drinks. As we sat upstairs, I asked if anyone was up there with us. Suddenly we heard movement and then quietness again. I started to ask another question, and this time we were positive that we heard movement, and it was coming from the attic! We did not know what to do as we could hear whatever was moving coming closer and closer to us. We sat there in fear not knowing if we should flee or sit there frozen. As our hearts began to pound in our chest, we then felt the bed move, and a loud meow echoed through the room! Laughter followed when we realized that a cat somehow got into the house, and that was what was causing all the racket. That was our extent of excitement for our time of seclusion.

Travis and Craig decided to hang out in the barn for a while so that the girls could investigate alone in the house. Kara, Savannah, and I headed upstairs and sat in the children's bedroom. We began with the ghost box, asking questions. Unfortunately, we did not realize that we were getting answers on the ghost box to our questions. Had we known that many of our questions were being answered we would have continued asking more and maybe we would have dug a little deeper. What we heard was just the sound of white nose that you get when no radio stations are coming through.

Upon going over our audio I began to hear the answers to the questions we were asking. First, I asked, "Who is up here with us?" The answer we received was very clearly "Lena." The answers to the first few questions were all the same voice, which sounded like a little girl's. I then asked if she wanted to go to bed, to which we received a response of "Lena... sleep." After a few more questions we decided to ask a few questions of the murderer to see if we would get any responses.

Once again, we did not hear the answers to our questions, but we heard them when we went over our audio. We asked the killer if the bloody water in the bowl on the table was used by him to clean the blood off his hands, to which we received a response of "yes." We then asked where he put his bloody clothes after the murder. He responded, "in the creek." I heard "took them with," so I said that out loud, and then he responded again "in the creek!" I then asked where he went after the murders, to which he responded, "to the cemetery."

I was amazed at the answers we received on the ghost box. If we were being told true answers, then we know that the killer cleaned his hands off in the bowl of water on the table, he threw his bloody clothes in the creek, and possibly he could have attended the funerals at the cemetery of his victims.

Who committed these horrific crimes over a hundred years ago, and why, will never be known. We ended our investigation at the cemetery where the Moore family, Lena and Ina are all buried, so that we could pay our respects to them. After all these years the mystery remains at the Villisca Ax Murder House. As we left Villisca, I did not feel like it was a goodbye, because I know that I will be back someday to investigate again.

The team at Villisca Ax Murder House

CHAPTER 11

WHISPERS ESTATE MITCHELL, INDIANA

By Craig Nehring

Whispers Estate

Whispers Estate was on my bucket list for a long time since it's listed as the most haunted place in Indiana and some guests had referred to it by saying they felt like a Gazelle at the watering hole and thought that something within the house was stalking them. We didn't have a big team for the weekend so we thought we would have some good activity with less people roaming the house on the investigation.

We had a two-night investigation planned here, and we could only investigate from 7:00 p.m. till 4:00 a.m. so I needed to find a place to stay close to the estate. I located something different as I don't like to always stay in hotels. I found Wilmstem cabins, which happened to be part of a safari in the town of Paoli that had tons of animals like bears and kangaroos. The cabin was neat looking and thought it would be cool to stay here for the two nights. We arrived to check in at the cabin with about an hour to spare. The cabin was situated in some trees across a little creek with a bridge. I kind of wished I had more time at the cabin.

The cabin where we stayed at in Paoli, Indiana

The History of Whispers Estate

Whispers Estate was built in 1894. In 1899 Dr. John and Jessie Gibbons purchased the house. Dr. John and Jessie Gibbons reportedly adopted abandoned/orphaned children. One of these children, a ten-year-old girl named Rachael, started a fire in the front parlor, was severely burned, and died two days later in one of the upstairs bedrooms. But you can still hear, and sometimes see, her running around the house today.

A ten-month-old infant, Elizabeth, died in the master bedroom of unknown causes, but there's still the scent of baby powder, and you can sometimes still hear her cries.

Jessie died in that same bedroom after a bout with double pneumonia. Guests sleeping in that room often awake to labored breathing and coughing. Some even report feeling as if someone is sitting on their chest. The most common paranormal activity in this room is with the closet doorknob, which will frequently jiggle for a few moments, stop suddenly, and the closet door will pop open.

Dr. Gibbons was a prominent doctor in town, having his office on the first-floor rooms in the house. Given the time period and medical field, it is likely many patients died there during his practice of twenty-six years.

Stories of subsequent owners suggest others have encountered their own demise, such as a gentleman in his fifties or sixties who died in the upstairs bathroom, and a young boy who died from falling down the front staircase.

In 2006, the previous owner bought the house after it was vacant for a few years. During its restoration, strange activity started to occur. Activity in the house continued, and even increased, subsequently earning the name 'Whispers Estate' after guests repeatedly reported hearing disembodied voices whispering in their ears.

Since 2006, the house has been investigated by numerous paranormal groups as well as visited by psychics and demonologists. It has been featured on numerous TV shows, multiple documentaries, specials, radio shows, and such.

There are supposedly four graves in the backyard, not including, what psychics have called a pit-grave, which they say contain amputated limbs, internal organs, aborted fetuses.

There is reportedly a portal/vortex that runs up through the house from the front parlor into the third floor room/attic. The room in the attic is said to be the heart of the house. Guests that are brave enough to sleep in this third floor room report horrible nightmares.

Visitors have reported sighting a shadow, which is now called 'Big Black', an entity that psychics say "is not of this world."

There are times when guests notice pleasant smells of baby power drift throughout the house, but the scent of pungent cologne, after-shave, cigar tobacco, rancid meat, cabbage, dirty medical bandages, and more are not uncommon.

Guest have reported their recording camcorders being moved by an unseen presence, thereby disturbing the viewpoint of the intended target.

The Tour of Whispers

We arrived at the estate and it was this massive white house that sat in front of us. We noted that the windows seemed to be darker than usual as you could see no light coming through at all. I called and the host answerd the phone and told us to come in and bring our equipment. We walked through the front doors and past the living room and into the dining room just off the kitchen. In the dining room was a place we could use as base camp. She showed us where the drinks were in the refridgerator if we got thirsty. We had everything ready to go for the tour and our first stop was the livingroom, which had a piano and some old photographs and a couple of couches. There were some cursed porcelain dolls on the piano, and she said not to touch them, or bad things would happen. I wasn't about to try the theory out and refrained from touching them. This room had a giant chandelier made of glass and she said that one time she was sleeping under it and it started shaking and swinging back and forth and thought it was going to rip from the ceiling. She had to move out from under it. This was also the room where the little girl accidently set herself on fire and she showed us the doors that slid closed to separate the room and the wood that was still scarred from the fire.

Our next stop was the laundry room, which at one point was where they did the abortions; just beyond that was the basement, which really didn't seem to have much activity at all. I said the furnace would be kicking all the time and it would be hard to hear stuff, so we decided to stick to the main house. There was one more bedroom off the corner of our base camp, which used to be the waiting room for the patients of the doctor. It now had some of the old medicine bottles that were found in the house along with some couches and an old light switch that you had to turn like a dial in order to get the room lights to turn on. On the backside of that room was where the doctor slept; some of the guests in the past were held down on this bed as it started to shake, the host told us. I said we would have to spend some time in there to see if it shook. There was a bathroom in there now but was once where he did the procedures; and to me it felt very normal, and I wasn't scared at all.

We then headed up to the second level and to the nursery area just before the stairs that led up to the attic area. It was here that I felt as though something was watching me in the dark. The host went on to tell us how one of the guests was dragged from the attic down to the bottom of that stairs and had to be taken to the hospital to get his face checked. He had a gash next to his eye and was bleeding and needed stiches. I have only seen that stuff happen on TV and was now feeling a little uncomfortable. She told everyone to hold the railing as we go up into the attic just in case something wanted to push us down the stairs. When we got to the top of the stairs there was a room that went to the left where there is supposed to be a vortex or portal in that room. There is a bed and a couch. The bed, is where someone was sucked into the bed or felt like they got sucked into the bed which reminds me of *Nightmare on Elm Street* where Johnny Depp gets sucked into his bed when he falls asleep. The couch across from the bed was where a police officer was taunting the ghosts because he didn't believe and was bitten by some unseen force that left bite marks. There was a mirror in pretty much every room, and now the host showed us a room that was called an Oculus room. It has mirrors on the floor and the ceiling and on every wall. This is said to be a way to communicate with ghosts since they can move between worlds with mirrors. I didn't try this out and don't think any of my team did either. I try not to dabble in things that I have no idea about and would worry what I might invite back into this world with me. The next room to the left had the heater in it and a metal frame bed with chairs around it. This bed will shake when you ask questions in the room and put your hands on it. The last room opposite the portal room was called the séance room where they hold seances. There was an Ouija board in this room and I counted like three or more boards in the house. I was even more uncomfortable now as our team won't use these devices and from what the host was telling us they seem to invite the negative spirits into the house. I was hoping we were not going to encounter any negative ghosts. I am OK with being scratched and stuff like that but the whole biting and getting tossed and dragged down the stairs is something I am not interested in.

One of the many Ouija boards in the house

The last stop on the tour was the floor that we skipped by the nursery to go up to the attic. This floor had two bedrooms and a bigger room with a staircase going down on the other side. The first bedroom was the doctor's wife's and she stayed in a different room and did not sleep with her husband. The next bedroom was Rachael's, the little girl who died due to the fire. I should note she didn't die in the fire since they brought her back up to her bedroom since she was severely burned. Her dress was melted into her skin by some reports and she laid in her bedroom in hopes her Dad could help her, but medicine back then was not like it is today with skin grafts and more. Her father gave her a shot of morphine to not only ease her pain from the burns but to put her out of her misery or mercy killing. In Rachael's room was tons of dolls and most of the dolls talk or sing and there are a few wind-up music boxes. The toys in this room tend to go off on their own and the only way to set the dolls off is to squeeze the dolls.

The dolls in Rachael's room

The final room to check out other than the bathroom was the last room down the hall; on one side there was a church pew that separated a kitchen area that had a curtain in front of it. The separation was because the floor was in poor shape in the kitchen, so they didn't want anyone walking in there. The other side of the room had a long closet and in that closet, was the table with some chair other teams have sat at. Those who would fall asleep in there would have terrible dreams, and they have also seen horned demons in that room as well. The host said that one team member saw the demon and yelled at it but it grabbed him and tossed him into the middle of the room. He was startled but unhurt. Well, the tour was done, and I was on edge thinking about what was instore for us tonight and tomorrow night. We headed back down to the base camp to get everything ready and grab a snack before we started.

The Investigation of Whisper's Estate

On the investigation was Melissa, Savanna, and myself. We were getting everything unpacked, and we had a couple of more things in the car to go get so Melissa and I walked toward the door but something came down the stairs next to us. It was loud footsteps walking right down next to us. I jumped and scared Melissa in the process, who said she heard them as well. I told Savannah this was going to be a good night since it was happening already. Our first stop was the attic since there seemed to be a lot happening up there in the past. We took the room where someone was sucked into the bed. Melissa and Savannah sat on the couch, and I stayed on the bed and started asking questions. It remained incredibly quiet. I thought I heard one loud footstep but that was all that was heard. We tried the room where the bed vibrates, and we tried the séance room, but nothing was heard. We headed down the stairs back to Rachael's room and sat in there for a little bit. There were some beach balls on the bed posts. I picked one up and tossed it on the floor; it came to a full stop and then it sounded like someone smacked it with their hand and it rolled back toward me. I jumped a little bit and that was all that happened in there.

We moved over to the pew area and the girls sat in the pew and I sat on a chair along the wall. The host said the ghost that resides in there don't like girls sitting on the pew and that they would poke them to make them move. We asked a bunch of questions but got nothing back, and they didn't seem to mind them sitting in the pew. We decided to take a break and gather some different equipment for round two.

Our next round we grabbed the thermal camera and the paranormal music box that plays music when ghosts get close to it. We wanted to try that in Rachael's room since she liked music. I set it close to her room but not quite in her room. I showed the ghosts what it sounded like and asked them to go by it. They didn't go by it but a doll in Rachael's room played something and we were not in the room when it happened, so we needed to walk to her room and check to see which doll had music coming from it. When we found the doll, we noted that it had to be wound up to play but heard it playing for longer than it could be wound up to. We stayed in her room for a bit since the doll played; we wanted to see if it would do it again, but it didn't. We heard a few small knocks and that was it. It was starting to get late, and we had a long drive down that day, so we decided to try two more rooms. We went to the doctor's office and the bedroom in there but there was no activity so we went back out to the living room to check it out and see if we could get the chandelier to move. The cursed dolls were in that room, and I reminded everyone to please not touch the cursed porcelain dolls and we didn't. While I am not superstitious, I still don't want to test fate. We didn't have any activity at all other than the doll playing music and some footsteps. I was rather surprised that all the hype that this house had as being the most haunted place in Indiana really wasn't living up to that name. We give tours and overnights at our asylum and that place was more active. Maybe we were just having a bad night and was hoping tomorrow night would be better.

Cursed dolls that reside at the estate

Night two and we are back at the estate hoping we capture something better than what we had the night before. I checked with a friend of mine who stayed here the week before and all he had was a few knocks and bangs and a few footsteps as well. We had a team that we are friends with staying here after us and they wanted the lowdown on what we get to see if they get things close to what we got.

We decided to start on the room by the cursed dolls and sat on the couches and started to ask questions like we always do. I thought I saw a black shadow descend the staircase and walk past this room toward the kitchen. I wasn't quite sure since it was pitch dark but thought I saw an outline. Was this Big Black that they talked about? The shadow didn't stop and didn't seem to be aware of us at all. We sat there for a while but heard nothing more. However the audio captured a voice saying, "Start to scare you." It was a EVP and was only captured on a voice recorder, so we didn't hear it at the time. We were not scared, and nothing more happened in that room. We moved on to the doctor's office and decided to lie on the bed to see if it would shake like some of the other guests had claimed. It was incredibly quiet in the room, and you could have heard a pin drop if someone tossed one. We had to create our own amusement and found ourselves laughing at something we were talking about. Maybe the ghosts would interact with us while we were making jokes. Still nothing happened and I said we should try the other rooms upstairs.

The bed in the doctor's office that shakes

We were now up in the bedroom in the attic hoping more would happen then the last night. There was nothing going on up here either; Savannah was even being a little sterner with the ghosts since asking them nicely wasn't getting any results but that wasn't working either. We were running out of options to try to get the ghosts to communicate. I said we should drop down one floor and try Rachael's room again, so we headed down there. I decided to lie in the mom's room next to her room and the two girls lay in Rachael's room to see what they could capture. They were asking questions in her room and the REM pod on the floor went off a few times but then all got quiet. I had nothing going on in my room at all. I got up and headed in by them and sat in the darkness. There was a noise down the hall by the pew area at the other end, but no more noises were heard in here. They said the REM pod went off a couple of times like maybe something stepped into the room and back out. We headed down to the pew area and I set the REM pod down and walked to the back area again while the girls sat down on the pew. The REM pod went off once for a couple of seconds and stopped. I thought either something came into the room or left the room but that was the last thing we heard. We headed back downstairs to take a break. We did one more round with no results and decided to call it a night. It was just after midnight but clearly nothing was happening there at all. All attempts to get all the ghosts that are there to communicate with us more went nowhere. We had a great time, and it was fun but our thoughts on the estate was that the host created all this fear. We have been doing this awhile now and were not scared. I often wonder if teams or groups that are new and never done this would be scared out of their wits at just the stories of the injuries that happened there, and any little bump or knock would terrify them. We had two incredibly quiet nights and the team before and afterwards saw little activity. My only concern with this place is evil is invited to come in and stay and I try to stay, away from horned things and bad mojo. I think the house is amazing inside but would wait to see if any other teams have more activity in the future.

CHAPTER 12

MOUNT MORIAH CEMETERY DEADWOOD, SOUTH DAKOTA

By Melissa Clevenger

Cemetery Fence Entrance

When Savannah and I began planning a trip to South Dakota, I never imagined how amazing it would be. This trip was a family trip with our two families, but somehow every trip we go on includes paranormal investigating in some way. We had an awfully long drive to South Dakota to discuss all our plans while we were there.

If this were a book on traveling, I would explain all the thrilling places that we went to in detail, but it is not; this is a book on the paranormal, so we will fast forward our trip to Deadwood. I love history, and Deadwood is full of history straight from the days of the Wild West. After spending our afternoon in Deadwood, we decided to go to Mount Moriah Cemetery. We arrived at 2:30 p.m. and the cemetery gates closed at 5:00 p.m., so we knew our investigating time would be short.

History of Mount Moriah Cemetery

Mount Moriah Cemetery in Deadwood, South Dakota, was established between 1877 and 1878. Deadwood originally had two graveyards, The Ingelside Cemetery and Mount Moriah Cemetery. As Deadwood began to grow it was decided that houses would work better where the Ingelside Cemetery was located. Work began to exhume the bodies from the Ingelside Cemetery and relocate them up the hill at Mount Moriah Cemetery. Unfortunately, in the early days gravesites were not marked very well, which caused many bodies or bones to be left behind. To this day home and business owners find bones of those left behind from Ingelside Cemetery when they are digging to put in basements or even garden work. The American flag flies over Mount Moriah Cemetery twenty-four hours a day, unlike most flags that fly from sunrise to sunset.

Mount Moriah Cemetery is the final resting place of many people who are well known from the Wild West. The most known buried here are Wild Bill Hickok, Calamity Jane, Potato Creek Johnny, and Seth Bullock. James Butler Hickok, known as Wild Bill, was murdered on August 2, 1876, when he was shot in the back of the head by Jack McCall. Martha Canary, known as Calamity Jane, died in 1903. Calamity Jane's dying wish was to be buried next to Wild Bill, and her wish was granted. Potato Creek Johnny claimed to have the biggest gold nugget to ever be found in the Black Hills; he died

February 21, 1943. Seth Bullock requested that he be buried facing Mount Roosevelt. It is quite a hike to get to his gravesite, which is about 750 feet above Mount Moriah.

The cemetery consists of many sections. The upper portion of the cemetery is where the Jewish section is located. There is a Chinese section that now only has a few graves remaining as most of the bodies were exhumed and returned to their families in China. In 1908, a burner and altar were constructed after representatives of the Chinese community were granted permission to install it. The burner and altar are where the largest number of Chinese were interred. The burner and altar were used according to their customs for offerings for the departed spirits.

The center of the cemetery is called the Masonic section and is known for the most elaborate headstones in the cemetery. Many of the early workers and settlers in Deadwood are buried in a section of the cemetery called Potter's Fields, which is filled with many unmarked graves of the unknown. There is also a section that is labeled as a mass grave site. The mass grave was for eleven men who died in a fire at a lumber mill that they were sleeping at. One section is labelled as the children's section. There was a large number of children dying from outbreaks such as cholera, smallpox, and typhus so they created a section in the cemetery for those children. Many Indian War and Civil War veterans are also buried in the cemetery, so there is a veteran's section for them.

Investigation of Mount Moriah Cemetery

We paid our fee to enter the cemetery with our investigating gear in hand and proceeded to the first gravesite that we wanted to investigate, Wild Bill Hickok. Wild Bill's gravesite was encased inside a rod iron fence. This was the most visited gravesite inside Mount Moriah, and this day was no different. Travis began to pull out the ghost box just as a trolly full of tourist pulled up on their tour of the cemetery. We casually sat there waiting for the trolly to move on with their tour.

Wild Bill's gravestone

Travis attached a speaker to the ghost box since we were out-
doors so that we could hear it better. For a moment, try to imagine
the song Kokomo sung by the Beach Boys. Do you have that song
in your head yet? We were sitting right by Wild Bills gravesite when
Travis hit the power button on the ghost box to see if we would
get any responses. Just as the power came on, another trolly full of
tourist pulled up, as the ghost box blared out the song Kokomo. As
Travis fumbled for the power button the song continued to play, and
we sat there completely mortified.

After the astonishment of what just happened passed us, we could
not help but laugh hysterically. The trolly moved on and we gave the
ghost box one more shot. We asked question after question with the
hopes of a response, but the ghost box was silent. We then moved on to
the next headstone over which was Calamity Jane's. So far, our investigation was not looking very well, and we had no evidence at all.

The next hour was spent walking from section to section of the
cemetery. The layout of this cemetery was like no other that I have been
to before. We visited the Jewish section, and then the Chinese section.

Chinese burner and altar

From there we paid our respects to all the kids that were buried in the children's section. We were getting our steps in with this cemetery and working out our calves with the treacherous hills.

From time to time, we would stop at random headstones and try the ghost box. We were beginning to run out of time and still had not gotten any evidence at all. As much as I had hoped to communicate with someone, I was still so impressed with this cemetery. In the distance we saw a large headstone that we were headed toward. Upon arriving, we decided to try the ghost box one last time.

I said hello, and instantly received the response of "hello." This was a pleasant surprise. I then asked who we were talking to, and the same man's voice simply replied "Franklin." We were shocked, and assumed this gentleman's first name was Franklin, that is until we looked up at the headstone and realized the last name Franklin on the headstone!

It was difficult to think of questions to ask because we knew nothing about this man whose last name was Franklin. We then asked "Mr. Franklin, what is your first name?" Surprisingly, the same man's voice responded with "Harris." We continued to get responses from Harris Franklin, but we were unable to determine exactly what he was saying. I then asked if he was married. Instantly on the ghost box we heard the name "Anna."

At this point we paused for a moment to see what names were around the Franklin headstone. There sat the plaque for Harris Franklin with the dates, March 20, 1849, to April 10, 1923. The next one that we saw was Anna Steiner Franklin March 27, 1849, to January 10, 1902. I could not believe it; Anna was Harris's wife and we heard that on the ghost box. We wished that we knew more about Harris since he was answering a lot of our questions.

We asked him if he had any children, to which he responded "one." We also heard him say "hotel." We thanked him for talking to us and told him to rest in peace. The time was now nearing 5:00 p.m. and we knew that the cemetery would soon be closing. It was now time to begin our long walk back to our vehicle.

That night in our hotel room, Savannah and I began to research the history of Harris Franklin. To our surprise, Harris Franklin was the owner of the very haunted Franklin Hotel located in downtown Deadwood! He was an extraordinarily successful businessman, and had a fortune from his liquor business; he also had ventures in banking, mining, and ranching. Harris and Anna had one child together. I was so glad that the one spirit that communicated to us we were able to find information on.

Harris Franklin's gravestone

Once I was able to process the history that we found on Harris Franklin and compare it to the answers we received from him at the cemetery, I was astonished at the accuracy. Mount Moriah cemetery is said to have 3,627 graves, although that number may be much higher due to lost records and incomplete information. Thousands of souls in one cemetery, and we had the pleasure to talk to one. We felt grateful for our experience because it is not often that you receive accurate information like this.

From the haunted streets of Deadwood to the desolate terrane of South Dakota, this was a family vacation that we would not forget. Sometimes the most haunted places are in the middle of nowhere, and if you are lucky enough, the ghost of the past may just pay you a visit.

CHAPTER 13

LEOPOLIS HAUNTED HOUSE
LEOPOLIS, WISCONSIN
By Craig Nehring

The Leopolis house that sits on the hill in town

I happened to know someone who knew the current owner of the Leopolis house and the townspeople referred to it as the haunted yellow house on the hill and people were afraid to get near it. It had a reputation for being haunted. We have been allowing teams to come and do investigations here now for a few years, and most of the teams that have come in have told us this is the most haunted place they have been too.

Leopolis is a small town that has two bars, a church, and a cemetery and is close to Shawano, Wisconsin. The house has three floors and a basement. There are lots of antiques in the house that the currant owner has collected over the years. I think many of the ghosts are attached to some of the stuff that sits in the house now. When you walk in the door you are greeted with a staircase that goes to the upper levels and a living room to the right side. The left side room has the dining room table that is an antique. I am not a fan of this table as the chairs sit straight up and make you lean forward. The kitchen is just beyond this with modern appliances. The living room on the other side has tons of furniture and is overcrowded with chairs and couches, which offers ample spots to sit but not much walking space. There is one back room off this room that has some more couches and may have one time been a sunroom area. The hallway that goes to the back of the house has a bathroom at the end and a staircase going downstairs with a few rooms that are overly cluttered. There is a room that might have once been a canning room and its small and square with shelves. The second floor has four bedrooms and a bathroom. The attic could be a finished room and is heated and reminds every one of the *Amityville Horror* house with the windows although they are not the same. I guess it just gives them that effect. There is a crawlspace in the attic, and I looked up there but there was not much room and nothing there. There is also a crawlspace by one of the walls, where lots of activity comes from as you will find out along the way in this story.

The outside of the house has a garage, and there was a rumor of a young girl committing suicide above the garage in a finished room; however, we can't find any documents pertaining to the suicide. Mediums that came to the property also confirmed this and said there were people buried on the property. A ghost box session not long ago that we used to communicate with the ghosts said that there were three men buried on the property. This has not been confirmed either. There was once a shed on the property that had some not so nice ghosts in it and some other buildings that have gone down in the windstorms. An investigator on another team had walked around the outside of the house and was scratched by something that left fingernail marks. He continued the investigation inside.

The History of Leopolis House

There is not much history on this house other than it was built in 1928 by a pig farmer who made money by farming to pay for the house. Some of the owners that had it in the 1970s have told us that it had lots of strange things going on in the house and that they would hear disembodied voices and noises from the house. There is a church next to the house that you can see out the window and a graveyard not too far away. It was an assisted living about ten years ago and that family stated it wasn't haunted at all. In years of doing this though we have encountered brand new houses that are haunted and houses that were never haunted that are now haunted. Just because a family never had a haunting in the house ten years ago doesn't mean it's not haunted now. I posted something about the house on one of my social media pages and was getting threats from the past owners about how we need to stop ghost hunting here, which makes me believe that this family is hiding something possibly even on the property. I will not heed their warnings, nor will I be bullied into doing so. They haven't lived there for ten years and don't own it, but it does throw red flags out there as to why they are so concerned about what we do with it. One of the current caretakers that moved in to watch the house since kids like to break into it had some stuff happen to him. He turned on a light and went to turn it off and the light stayed on even though the switch was off, and it slowly and gradually got dimmer till it was out. The owner told him it's a different type of electricity to make him feel at ease rather than telling him the truth. He also had a remote fly off his TV set without warning although he thinks the TV was sitting on an angle and it rolled off, but I am sure he wanted to make himself feel better. He since has a dog, which I am sure calms his fears in the house.

The Investigations

During one of our first investigations there, we were sitting in the room with all the furniture, and we had closed the glass doors leading to the other room and the kitchen as well as the stairway leading upstairs. We were having fun and joking around before we started the investigation, and Richard, the current owner, was telling us a story of how he had antlers in the place from deer; when someone wanted to move the antlers, growls were heard from within the room and they asked him what to do with the antlers and he said to get rid of them now. They did and we wonder if that is why some of the ghosts are active there because they are missing now. While he was telling us this story, we heard what sounded like footsteps coming down the stairs from the second floor. We knew that everyone was in the room and no one was upstairs. The footsteps stopped at the bottom by the closed glass doors. I walked up to the door and slowly opened one of them. When I opened the door, something moved and ran back up the stairs back to the second floor. It startled me as I could see nothing there. I walked back into the room and everyone's eyes were wide and they had heard the footsteps too. I grabbed a REM pod and put it at the bottom of the stairs and sat back in the room with everyone else. We were not sitting in there long when the pod started going off, which meant something was by it and I walked over to check it out and something grabbed the back of my sweatshirt and I spun around to see who it was. There was nothing there and clearly something had pulled it and was still in at the bottom of the stairs and close to us. Nothing was heard after that, and we decided to head upstairs to the attic to see what might be in there.

We sat on some of the chairs in the attic and pulled out the ghost box to run white noise and talk to them. The voices that came through were clear and said a few names like Janet and Anne and said three men were buried out back. We also heard something get tossed in the attic like a rock, and I turned off the device and another rock was tossed at us. I picked it up to see what kind of rock and found it to be a bead and not a rock. It was beads off maybe a necklace or something like that. It happened a couple of times and they were all beads but where were they coming from? We didn't have the answer for that. Some of the other investigators were touched here as well and had their hair pulled. We were there most of the night and heard lots of loud knocks and bangs but had to leave to head home. But we would come back soon.

It has been awhile since we had done any investigations here, but many teams have rented it out for the night. It was now time for us to come back in, only this time we were spending the night since the owner now had beds guests could sleep on. I picked the one room where kids like to open the closet door, or we think they are kids at least. On the investigation was John, Kara, Brittnie, Nikki, and myself. We started like we always do siting around a table talking to the owner of the house and snacking and telling stories. Nikki had joined us on this investigation from Annik Paranormal. I wanted to see how she investigated since she would be helping at the asylum this year on our events.

Our first stop was the attic and we all sat down in the chairs and now there was a couch up there as well. I along with John and Kara were in chairs along the wall and Kara was right in front of the creepy crawlspace. I had a thermal camera but wasn't picking anything up on it, so I turned it off. I told Brittnie who was on the couch to use the ghost box, so she pulled that out and turned that on. I heard some voices come through. A name was repeated and the name was Pablo, one that I haven't heard before here. It was dark other than the constant scanning of the white noise. I jumped a little as something had grabbed my fingers on my hand and it felt like cold icy fingers on my own. It was confirmed on the ghost box when something stated they had grabbed me and then it said touched and I then felt something touch my shoulder. I turned on the flashlight and saw nothing as usual. We continued when suddenly Kara jumped up screaming that it felt like something jammed a long sharp object into her side and she was a little shaken. The ghost that resides in the attic I thought might be kids as in the past I have heard a little girl say that she used to play up there and there were some drawings on the ceiling that looked like a dog.

Picture of dog on the ceiling in the attic

We continued now as Kara sat back down and turned on the ghost box again. Voices on it were saying "I am headed your way" and "crawlspace." We heard what sounded like two loud knocks on the crawlspace door in the attic and then something scratching like it wanted to get out. I thought it could be an animal and I had someone open the door to look but nothing was in there and we know that scratches came from on the door. I decided to knock on the wall and tell them to knock back and something again knocked back. We heard some noises coming from down on the lower level and possibly a footstep coming up the stairs to the attic. Just as that happened John screamed out that something had kicked him, and it wasn't any of us. We didn't hear any more on the ghost box but all three of us who were along the crawlspace door had something happen now.

The crawlspace in the attic

We didn't hear anything else in the attic, so we headed downstairs again to first floor to see what was happening down there. We sat at the main table in the dining room and put a few K2s on the table, which are devices that pick up energy should a ghost be in the room with us. They also pick up electrical currents so they need to be away from outlets and cell phones that can make them go off. The devices started to go off to our questions and it was on cue. We asked if the ghosts liked the caretaker that lived there, and it didn't light up but when we asked if they didn't like him it went up to red. I wanted to make sure this is what they meant so we asked the same questions once again and it lit up the same way. We won't be telling the caretaker so if he reads this then he will know. For some of the investigators it was getting late, and they needed to leave but I was going to be staying the night with the ghosts. Richard was leaving too and taking the dog with him, which meant I was alone in the house with whatever ghosts were just causing havoc in the attic. I slept in the room where the closet door opened. I checked in there before hopping into bed and it had tons of stuff in there. I put a table in front of it to keep it from opening as I really wanted to sleep and not wake up to it opening. It wasn't a bad night but I did hear some loud footsteps and some knocking on my room door. I wondered if they wanted me to say "come on in." Why would they knock if they could go where they want but maybe were being polite. I will have to go back in the future and stay the night again and see what happens. This is one place guests can stay the night for a fee and see what happens to them while sleeping here.

Nikki, John, Craig, Brittnie, and Kara

CHAPTER 14

Fox Hollow Farm
Carmel, Indiana

By Melissa Clevenger

Fox Hollow Farm in Carmel, Indiana

The life of a serial killer is something that we will never understand. Their inner demons are so fierce that the thought of their gruesome attacks terrifies us to the core. It is somewhat natural to be fascinated by them; we try to understand their world and make sense of what they have done. The acts of serial killers are something that our minds cannot comprehend, which causes us to be curious.

Fox Hollow Farm was right at the top of my bucket list locations that I wanted to investigate, so we set out to make it happen. I had extremely high hopes for this investigation and could not wait to get there. We knew that one night of investigating would go extremely fast, so we planned out our night the best we could.

Along the way we stopped in an incredibly unique city named Carmel, Indiana. I immediately fell in love with Carmel as we took funny pictures with every human-looking statue along the sidewalks. The highlight of our stop, other than the statues, was nitrogen ice-cream at Sub Zero. This was the best ice-cream that I have ever tasted in my life! Next stop, Fox Hollow Farm.

The statues around town in Carmel

Kristin, Melissa, Savannah, and Craig

The History of Fox Hollow Farm

Herb Baumeister opened two Save-A-Lot thrift stores in the 1980s. By 1991, Herb and his wife, Julie, had saved enough money to buy their dream home. Their new home Fox Hollow Farm was 11,000 square feet sitting on 18 acres. The house with 5 bedrooms and an indoor pool was perfect for their family with their 3 children.

Herb was often left alone at the house while Julie and the kids would go to the family's lake home. This created the perfect opportunity for Herb to carry out his fascinations. He began to spend his nights scoping out the Indianapolis gay scene. Herb would go to the gay bars under the alias of Brian Smart with the hopes of taking unknowing victims back to Fox Hollow Farm to party.

Before long gay men began disappearing without a trace from the Indianapolis area. Unfortunately, many of these men went unnoticed due to societies view on them at that time. In the early 1990s, a man named Roger Goodlet vanished and his friend Tony Harris was determined to figure out what had happened to him.

One night Tony was at the local gay bar when he noticed a man oddly sitting staring at the missing poster for Roger. Tony approached the man who addressed himself as Brian Smart. With hesitation, Tony decided to leave with Brian to go to his boss's estate. After driving down some long dark curvy roads, the two men came up to Fox Hollow Farm.

Brian and Tony went straight to the indoor pool where they began to engage in sexual activity. Tony found it odd that the pool area was filled with mannequins with many of them in different positions. Brian explained that his boss did not like to feel alone which was why the mannequins were there.

Soon a session of autoerotic asphyxiation followed. Tony knew that something was wrong, and he felt that this was how his friend Roger was killed. Tony then confronted Brian accusing him of killing his friend to which Brian laughed and said no one would believe him with his accusations. We will never know why, but Brian let Tony go without killing him.

Tony immediately contacted the police explaining that Brian Smart was strangling and killing gay men in the area. The police began to investigate the killings but were quickly sidelined when nobody came up with the name of Brian Smart. Soon after Tony saw Brian in the same bar again, he was able to follow him to his vehicle where he could write down a license plate number. The license plate number traced to Herb Baumeister.

When Herb was first visited by detectives questioning his involvement and his frequent visits to the gay bar scene, Herb instantly appeared to panick. When asked if authorities could search the Fox Hollow Farm property, Herb refused the requests. Law enforcement then went to Julie to gain access for the search. She insisted that her husband was not guilty, and the investigators would need to produce a warrant to search the property.

Unfortunately, due to the lack of evidence and simple accusations from Tony, the officials were unable to produce a warrant. Before long, Julie filed for divorce. Later it came out that Herb's son at one point found a skull in the woods. He brought the skull to his mom to show her. Upon inspection she went out to the woods where she found several other bones.

Julie presented the finding to Herb, to which he explained that these were model skeletons of his fathers. Herb then proceeded to bury those skeletons in the woods. This was before the authorities came to the house, so at the time when this occurred Julie accepted Herb's answer as the truth and thought no more of it.

Detectives were contacted with this new information about the bones, and then were finally able to conduct a search of the property. To their shock, their search found bones scattered throughout the property. The detectives found larger bones toward the back of the woods, and smaller bones buried and burned toward the front of the woods directly behind the house.

Authorities were able to find the remains of eleven victims on the property and were able to identify eight of those. One of the victim's identified was that of Roger Goodlet, whose disappearance started the investigation in the first place.

It is believed that Herb Baumeister may have killed up to twenty-seven men, and according to Tony possibly closer to fifty men. During the 1980s there was a serial killer known as the I-70 strangler who had killed nine men along this stretch of I-70. Law enforcement believed that Herb Baumeister could have been responsible for those killings as well.

Upon the discovery of bones on the Fox Hollow Farm property, Herb Baumeister fled to Canada. On July 3, 1996, Herb was found dead from a self-inflicted gunshot wound. He had a three-page suicide letter sighting his failed marriage, his failed business, and his children. In the letter there was no mention at all of the murders that he had committed.

The Investigation of the Fox Hollow Farm

Our investigation would include Craig, Travis, Savannah, Kristin, and myself. We arrived at Fox Hollow Farm at 7:00 p.m. to meet with Rob Graves the owner of the house. With my first step out of the vehicle, I was amazed by the beautiful house. It was hard to wrap my head around the horrific crimes that had taken place on the property.

Once we brought all our equipment into the house, Rob Graves began to take us on a tour of the house and property. His tour included stories and history about every inch of the property. It was a very intriguing and fascinating tour, and I was excited to begin our investigation. I noted the hotspots that Rob told us about, which included the burn pit, mulch pit, the creek where all the bone fragments were found, Rob's bathroom, the pool area, bar, and the apartment.

Our first stop on our tour were the woods behind the house where the bodies were disposed of. My intuition and psychic abilities were strong on this investigation. While walking along the path I was pulled toward a large sycamore tree. Intuitively I was told that there was a body laid to rest there that had not been found. At the same time Savannah heard someone say to her to "look up or you won't see." I did not say anything to Rob about the sycamore tree and shortly after this instance, Rob directed us to that very tree to talk about it.

Once our tour was complete, we decided to begin our investigation in the woods behind the house. For this part of the investigation, we decided to only use a voice recorder and the ghost box for equipment. We began with a ghost box session where we asked several questions of the victims and of Herb Baumeister. We asked who was there, and we received a noticeably clear response of "Herb." We continued to get Herb several more times across the ghost box. At one point Kristin felt something grab her arm. I asked, "Who grabbed Kristin's arm just now?" Once again, the answer "Herb" came across the ghost box.

I then asked, "What is in the woods back her?" Upon going over my audio I heard the answer to my question. The response to my question was, "my body parts… hurt him." I then asked, "Who did this to you?" Once again, the response on the ghost box was "Herb." Next, I asked "Is Herb still trying to hurt people?" On the ghost box we heard a man's voice reply with "yes," and yet another voice said "help." We were getting answers to our questions that were extremely specific and we were not getting much interference.

The woods behind the house where bones were found

After the woods, Savannah and I wanted to see the apartment while the others were setting up the DVR system. The door into the apartment led us directly into the kitchen and to the right of that was a door that I felt drawn to. Upon opening the door, we realized that it was to a closet. Savannah and I both felt that we needed to sit in the closet for a little bit and ask a few questions. At this time, we had no equipment on us other than our phones for taking pictures.

We both began to have a heavy feeling in our heads and almost felt like we had both been drugged. I had a sharp stabbing pain on the left side of my head and a headache. Savannah also began to have a sharp stabbing pain on her head but on the right side. We began to feel very uneasy and scared, almost like we were trapped in the closet. As our fear heightened, Savannah's phone started taking pictures without her touching it.

We began to feel even more panicked by this time. Something just did not feel right in that closet. Her camera then continued to take pictures on its own. I said we needed to get out of there! Just then Savannah's phone began to take a burst of pictures. Almost like hundreds of microbursts of pictures without us touching it. At this point the energy in the closet was so intense and out of shear panic Savannah screamed pushing me out of the closet.

Once we regained our composure, we decided to inspect Savannah's phone and see what pictures we captured. We both knew that there should be at least a hundred pictures just from our time in the closet. To our amazement there was only one picture taken in the closet. I could not understand what happened, but I knew that the closet was a place full of energy that frightened us both.

After our somewhat terrifying experience we decided to join our group once again. Travis and Craig decided they would investigate the pool area first while the girls went back to the apartment with equipment. In the pool area Travis and Craig heard footsteps coming toward them as they sat by the pools edge. At one point they heard us girls coming down the stairs. They even heard our voices coming closer, only to realize that we were nowhere around to be heard.

Travis and Craig then decided to investigate in the pump room. The pump room is where the pool hose was kept that Herb would use to strangle his victims in the pool. On the voice recorder a man's voice says "a**hole." Shortly after they begin to use the ghost box and a man's voice says, "a**holes are sitting there." I am not sure if this was in reference to Craig and Travis, but it seemed that someone was agitated that they were in there. One other voice was picked up in the pool room, but we were unable to distinguish what was said.

Savannah, Kristin, and I continued our investigation in the apartment area while the guys were in the pool area. As we sat quietly in the living room area, we heard something move loudly in the kitchen. We continued to hear footsteps and various noises coming from the kitchen. We got the name "Eddy" several times on the ghost box and what is interesting is that the guys also got that name a few times. We then decided to try the closet once again.

The three of us reluctantly proceeded into the closet and closed the door behind us. We felt very vulnerable in there, but at least we were not alone. Instantly, the three of us all began to feel like we were drugged. It was remarkably like what Savannah and I had experienced in there before. Our heads were heavy, and we were all dizzy. The investigation must go on though, so we continued to investigate and ask questions. We felt a presence of a young boy in the apartment who was possibly killed there. We felt like he was not yet sixteen and possibly disowned by his parents. This was just a feeling though and not a fact that we can prove.

We captured an EVP in the closet when we asked what happened in there that said, "We were f***ing." We did uncover several explicit words on our voice recorder that night. Going over my audio I also picked up what sounded like crying in the closet. We all began to feel uneasy after a short while and we needed once again to get out of the closet. After standing outside of the closet for a while, I was looking in and a section of clothes began swaying back and forth. At this same time, I picked up the same crying sound on my recorder again.

The pool in Fox Hollow

Next, we decided to investigate the pool area and Craig and Travis went up to the apartment to investigate. Savannah sat by the edge of the pool with her entire leg in the water, while Kristin and I both stuck our arms in the water. We felt that this would bring our energy into the pool. We heard several voices, splashes of water, and footsteps while we sat there quietly. We then noticed a bright glowing ball of light just above the water. I tried to debunk it as a light shining in, but I had no way to explain this light and its brightness it was not natural.

I took several pictures in the water, and Savannah then said she felt like something was on her leg. At this exact moment I snapped a picture where there was a large glowing light surrounding her leg. Savannah had broken her leg in five places prior to this so it did not surprise me that this light appeared around her leg as possibly the spirits could feel her pain. We heard noises coming from the supply room by the pool. It was a shuffling sound that proceeded to shuffle closer to us, and then we began to hear splashes coming from the center of the pool. Instantaneously the three of us pulled out of the water at the same time.

The light by Savannah's foot in the pool

We then heard Travis and Craig talking and coming down the stairs. It seemed like the perfect time for them to come since the pool area was beginning to get highly active. Travis' voice began to get closer to the bottom of the stairs, so we figured they were ready to investigate as a group.

I turned on my flashlight so that they would know to come into the pool area with us. I stood up to walk to the pool room doorway to greet them and ask how their investigation in the apartment went. I could still hear them talking as I peeked around the corner and peered toward the stairs. To my surprise nobody was there; in fact, no one was anywhere around. The guys were still in the apartment.

Hearing the guys talking and coming down the stairs ended up happening several more times as we sat in the pool room. On my audio I picked up a soft yell followed by a weird sound that I cannot describe. Once the guys finally came down and joined us, we investigated the bar area as a group.

In the bar area I asked if they could tell me what happened to them? On my voice recorder we received an answer in a man's voice that said, "I am about to." While we were using the ghost box, it said that there was a secret portal there. I do not know if this is true or even how to find out about a secret portal. A voice on the ghost box then says, "Trying to maybe bring us back," followed by a man's voice that says "yes." It is so sad to think of the victims, and them saying "trying to maybe bring us back" is truly heartbreaking.

To end our night Craig, Travis, and Kristin investigated Rob's bathroom while Savannah and I investigated the woods alone. As Travis stepped through the doorway of the bedroom, he saw a full body apparition walk by the dresser right by him. It looked like a real person and the clothes were in color. The apparition walked by, stopped, turned and walked through the door. It took Travis a moment to realize that nobody was there, and this was not a real person that he had just seen.

The bathroom where the apparition was seen

In the woods Savannah and I turned off our lantern and stood there in the complete darkness. There then was a very loud stomp that came from right in front of us. There was an EVP of a voice that said several sentences very quietly; however, I was not able to determine what was said. We proceeded to talk to the victims of Herb Baumeister, and to tell them how sorry we were for what had happened to them and that they did not deserve that. The woods began to feel very peaceful and calm.

Normally when a haunted location is on your bucket list and you finally have the opportunity to investigate it, you would mark it off your bucket list. Fox Hollow Farm is my exception to that rule as it is still on my bucket list. I feel that there is still so much to investigate and learn from the property. In closing I will leave you with our final EVP from Fox Hollow Farm: a voice that simply said, "Tell them everything."

CHAPTER 15

SHEBOYGAN INSANE ASYLUM SHEBOYGAN, WISCONSIN

By Melissa Clevenger and Craig Nehring

The Sheboygan Insane Asylum

Our team the Fox Valley Ghost Hunters is now beginning our third year conducting ghost investigations at the Sheboygan Insane Asylum. We are the only paranormal team with exclusive access to the property. Over the past three years, we have investigated the building well over a hundred times. As a team we can all say that this is one of the most haunted locations that we have ever investigated.

On any given night we do not know what to expect in the asylum. When we are giving tours to the public, one tour can be completely quiet, and the very next may be extremely active. We always hope for an active night, but there is never a guarantee. This is one thing that we love about the asylum, that we just never know what to expect.

The History of the Sheboygan Insane Asylum

In 1876, the Sheboygan County Asylum for the Insane was completed. The asylum began with eight patients that were being kept at the county jail as there was no suitable place to house them. Not long after opening it housed forty patients. Then on February 19, 1878, a fire broke out at the facility killing four of the patients. Of the four patients who passed away, one was listed as Billy Doe, an idiot, whose name was unknown.

Rebuilding of the asylum began almost immediately. The building was completed and fully furnished on June 1, 1882. As the years passed on, the need for more land to house the growing number of patients was imminent. Larger sections of land were purchased so that the asylum could continue to grow.

In 1938, the asylum was relocated to land about 3 miles from Sheboygan Falls. The new location could sustain 350 people and included a working farm that would become known as the poor farm. The building consisted of Y-shaped wings with men on the north side and women on the south. Nurses would be housed onsite due to the rural location of the asylum. There was a separate boiler house and underground tunnels were used to enclose pipes and wiring.

On April 14, 1940, the new Sheboygan County Comprehensive Health Care Center opened its doors. Glazed tile walls were used throughout the building so the staff could hose down the walls and floors for easy cleaning. Several years later a library, barber shop, beauty shop, fashion boutique, and a chapel were added to the building.

Forty-three German prisoners of war were housed to work at the asylum in 1945. By 1963, the asylum had about 295 patients that included mentally deficient, mentally ill, and the mentally infirmed. From 1969 until 1978, the facility offered drug and alcohol rehabilitation. '

In 1978, the mentally ill services were discontinued, and it became a county home for the developmentally disabled and chronically ill. By December 2002, the building shut its doors and was put up for sale.

The Investigation of the Sheboygan Insane Asylum

These are some of our best moments at the asylum ranging from scary to extreme fear. We do not believe that any of the ghosts that are at the asylum are stuck there; they simply seem to enjoy our company and the chance to communicate with us. It is not uncommon to hear bangs, knocks, and voices here. You may even see a shadow figure or full body apparition.

On one cold night we did a small team investigation and began getting activity on the second floor. We typically investigate down the long halls in the wings, but this night we decided to investigate in the opening between the four wings. Down the left wing we heard a loud bang. As we began to walk toward the bang; another bang in the opposite direction caught our attention. Soon the bangs began on either side of us. We could not figure out what was causing the loud bangs and noises, but we knew that we should stay where we were.

Before long, the bangs got so loud that Travis decided to go down the left wing, while Craig went down the right wing. Lynzi and I stood there in the dark not knowing what to do. I then yelled out "hello" into the darkness. Suddenly, we both heard the voice of a man clearly say "hi." The voice came from directly behind us. We were startled but intrigued to ask more questions. When the four of us finally regrouped, the bangs were no longer down the wings but were coming from right beside us.

On another night we had just completed doing our public investigation. By now it was 2:30 a.m., and I realized that we had forgotten a table and a chest of trigger items down the first-floor wing. Craig and Travis stayed in the lobby; while Lynzi, Jordyn, and I went to retrieve the stuff.

Travis and Melissa hear loud bangs

The building was completely quiet and empty besides us. Although the items we were retrieving were only on the first floor, it seemed like a long way to walk. As I began to pick up the chest, I decided that the three of us should do a little investigation. Jordyn was already scared, so I told her that we could all three sit next to each other against the wall. Nothing to be scared of, just three investigators in a big dark building alone.

Things escalated very quickly for us, and this soon became the first time I have ever ran in fear. I began by asking whoever was with us to open the chest that was down the hall from us. Jordyn immediately said, "If that chest opens, I am out of here." Before I even had a chance to laugh at her remark, we heard a scrapping sound coming from the next wing over.

The sound of something scrapping the cement floor instantly made us alert. As our heads tilted to listen, the bloodcurdling scream of a woman began. In a sheer panic, Jordyn flew in the air and was down the hall. Lynzi followed suit, chasing after Jordyn. I was still sitting, frozen in shock at what was happening.

The scream continued, a constant shrill, ear-piercing scream. I shouted for them to come back for me, and to not leave me there. Lynzi ran back, and I made her grab the table as I ran to grab the chest. Lynzi dragged the table behind her running, as I ran holding the chest tightly. We finally made it to where Jordyn was jumping in the air waving her arms for us to hurry.

We finally reached the door that would let us into the hall before the lobby. Several minutes had passed, yet the shrill scream continued through this all. The second Jordyn's hand grabbed the door, the scream ceased. As scared as we were, we never screamed through this entire experience.

As we ran into the lobby where the guys were, Travis immediately asked, "What were you guys screaming at?" Travis and Craig heard the scream all the way in the lobby area! I still wake up some mornings and I can distinctly hear the scream from that night in my head. I never thought that I would run on an investigation, but in this instance, I really did not know what to do. If this happens again, I am determined to investigate further and maybe get some answers.

The hallway where the scream was heard

Craig's Encounters with the Asylum Ghosts

I have had many encounters with the things that go bump in the night in the asylum. The night we opened the morgue for the first time by pounding a hole in the wall to gain access, all hell broke loose. Not sure what was left inside there or why, all at once there was more activity as though something was released and not too happy with us. I had a ghost tour that night and there seemed to be a darkness surrounding the morgue area. We went past there on the tour and some even peeked in there but not for too long. We headed up to the chapel to talk to a ghost we call Hope, who likes to reside in that area. We turned on the ghost box and Hope was there, but there was something more there that night. Voices came through and said "evil" and "demon." Now this is nothing new and it happens quite a bit since they like to tell us things we are afraid of. I remember standing against the back wall and feeling like someone had just punched me hard in my lower back. I had someone look and it was red in color and the pain lasted for a little while before going away. I recovered from that and asked who had punched me and a voice came through that said, "I did." I wasn't about to leave so we stayed there longer when something scratched me on my arm, and it left red marks down my arm. I decided to move from that location and had one of the other tour guides lead so I could go back to base camp and relax for a little bit.

It wasn't long after that I heard lots of voices heading my way and wondered why they were done so quickly. They needed a break too as one of the girls was scratched on the leg and another guy got punched in the eye by something. Everyone was OK and they continued for the rest of the tour. I didn't have anything else happen to me the rest of the night.

One evening while doing a ghost tour I was in one of the many wings on the third floor when we heard lots of noise coming from the other end of the hallway like loud bangs and footsteps maybe in the stairwell at the other end. I walked down about halfway to see if I could hear more. I asked for whatever was there to come and say hi to me. I now know the saying "be careful about what you wish for." Just after I said for them to come by me, there were loud footsteps that came down the hall and right up to me and stopped right in front of me. I put my hand out and it felt cold, but I couldn't feel anything except this cold spot. I backed up a little bit and heard it take another step closer to me. I walked back to the group a little quicker, but it didn't follow. Maybe they thought too many people were there to continue. We then set up a laser grid to try to see if anything would cross the grid and we had some REM pods down at the other end. We didn't have to wait too long before one of the REM pods went off letting us know something was there; the red lines from the grid were breached by a dark shadow. Some of the guests said they saw enough and wanted to leave the building so one of the guides walked them back to the entrance where they left never to be seen in the building again. The rest of the brave souls stayed on to watch if anything more would happen.

The chapel area where Craig was punched and scratched

We pulled out the ghost box and I yelled "Marco" and something yelled "Polo" back to us. There was also a little girl that all of us heard saying that her favorite color was purple. I turned off the device just in time to capture a loud noise at the end of the hall like someone was dragging something heavy down the hall. It was followed by the sounds of a little girl giggling and then singing but we didn't know what tune she was singing. Some guests wondered why there were children there and I noted there, was a swing set out back. There were reports of children on the property from time to time.

The swing sets for children

It was quiet, and we had all the guests leave, and now I had to go lock the building by myself since everyone left. I got to the end of the tunnels to lock one of the doors that run between them, and as the door was closing, I heard a loud shriek come from in the tunnel; it didn't sound too pleasant. I quickly made the door close faster than it wanted to and locked it behind me knowing that whatever was in there surely could just walk through the door without a second thought. I still felt safer. I walked a little quicker back to the stairs leading to the second floor and thought I heard footsteps behind me and shined my light in the direction, but nothing was there. I made it to second floor and locked the rest of the doors and headed outside to my car. I had this odd feeling outside by my car that I needed to look up at the window, which was a bad mistake. When I looked up to the floor that I thought something had followed me; there was a bright flash of light and a dark figure that was in the window for a split second—gone as fast as it appeared. I had a hard time sleeping that night after I got home.

The final story I want to share happened in 2020 at the end of the year around October. We had Lynzi, Jordyn, Khyla, and myself on the team leading the tours. It was an active night and one of the girls on my team was so scared of one of the ghosts that reside in the asylum that she wouldn't go alone to lock the doors on the next level. She says it's a negative entity, which it could be, but nothing has ever harmed us other than scratches and stuff that don't need medical attention. That night after the tours we decided to investigate a little bit more without all the guests so we went to the third floor and to the right in one of the wings and the girls sat in the middle on the floor back-to-back so they could watch all sides. We started asking questions to see if Hope was with us or wanted to talk. We heard footsteps in the distance and knocks close to us but out of reach. It was almost if something was trying to get close but still at arm's length. I was videotaping this little escapade and was standing facing down the hallway when suddenly something grabbed me from behind. I wasn't expecting it and spun around in terror, and the girls all jumped and screamed and asked what happened. I said something had grabbed me. The girls asked a few questions when we all heard something yell out to us from the hall, but to me it sounded more like a scream for a second. Now there seemed to be something getting closer to us, and Lynzi on our team put out her hand and asked Hope to come over to her. There was a dark figure in the hall in front of us and my video camera wouldn't focus on it at all. We all said that was not Hope but something else and the air felt heavy, and everything seemed dark. The girls said we need to leave now because whatever this thing was it didn't seem nice. I could have stayed to investigate more but knew they were scared, and some were even shaking. As we were leaving to go downstairs and away from whatever was up there, I captured a voice on my video camera that said, "Choke them." I am glad I didn't hear that till I got home and went over audio since the only ones there to choke was us. We look forward to meeting new guests on our tours here this year and in the future.

The team in the hallway of the asylum

CHAPTER 16

A New Beginning
By Melissa Clevenger

What are your thoughts when you first drive through the gates of a cemetery? Do you reminisce about the memories from your own loss or do you think of how lucky you are to be alive? I often wonder if my loved ones are in the car with me, as I drive to visit their gravesite. I can only imagine them resting their hand on my shoulder as I shake my head in sadness.

Upon entering the gates of Cave Hill Cemetery in Louisville, Kentucky, I was instantly in awe over the sheer beauty. It felt like each headstone told a part of that person's life. As we drove down every twist and turn, I was captivated over the expression of love that was put into each gravesite. In the 1800s the grounds were known as the "City of the Dead." Within the cemetery there are five lakes and a quarry, and well over 138,000 people buried there.

Our first stop was the gravesite of Muhammad Ali. Tiny red roses and little yellow flowers led up the steps to where Muhammad Ali was laid to rest. One single red rose lay just below his name.

I had the honor of meeting Muhammad Ali when I was a teenager. I had boarded an airplane all alone from Kansas City, Kansas, on my way to visit my mother in Wisconsin. Before I was able to take my seat, I was knocked over by an exceptionally large duffle bag. That duffle bag was held by Muhammad Ali himself. He apologized immensely before taking his seat in front of me. I did not, however, know who this man was until I got off the airplane. What I did know though was that he was a very polite and kind man.

Muhammad Ali's grave

We then ventured to the gravesite of Colonel Harland Sanders. Colonel Sanders was the founder of the Kentucky Fried Chicken empire. His headstone almost looks like the front of the White House with four pilers, and a statue of his head in the middle. To me, this headstone is a reminder to work hard and never give up on your dreams.

Colonel Sanders' gravestone

One by one we visited some of the most elaborate headstones. Inscribed on one headstone was, "I am the rock in your garden, you are the flower in mine." These were such beautiful words to be spoken. The love of this couple will forever be inscribed for all to see. Further down the road was another headstone that told the story of a true love. A man and his wife eternally dancing.

Upon the top of the next one that caught my eye was a man's hand, and he was handing his wife some flowers. I can only imagine that this was something he did for her often when they were alive. With one simple headstone, a beautiful story unfolds.

The cemetery is a stern reminder to cherish your loved ones who are still with you. Live your life and be an inspiration to others. It is also a reminder to me of why I am a paranormal investigator. Once our loved one's pass, we are only left with their memories that they left behind. I find peace when spirits communicate with us, as it reassures me that my loved ones are also still around. What we call the end, is merely a new beginning.

The couple forever dancing even after death

Husband handing wife flowers

A new beginning

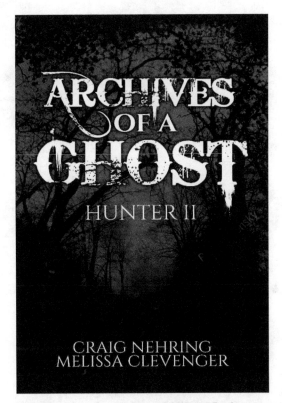

Find our last book from 2020 on Lulu.com

Melissa Clevenger and Craig Nehring

CPSIA information can be obtained
at www.ICGtesting.com
Printed in the USA
LVHW080945210921
698338LV00009B/128